C0-GLV-452

THE RELIGIOUS DROP-OUTS

Volume 44, Sage Library of Social Research

SAGE LIBRARY OF SOCIAL RESEARCH

1. **David Caplovitz:**
The Merchants of Harlem
2. **James N. Rosenau:**
International Studies and the Social Sciences
3. **Douglas E. Ashford:**
Ideology and Participation
4. **Patrick J. McGowan and Howard B. Shapiro:**
The Comparative Study of Foreign Policy
5. **George A. Male:**
The Struggle for Power
6. **Raymond Tanter:**
Modelling and Managing International Conflicts
7. **Anthony James Catanese:**
Planners and Local Politics
8. **James Russell Prescott:**
Economic Aspects of Public Housing
9. **F. Parkinson:**
Latin America, the Cold War, and the World Powers, 1945-1973
10. **Robert G. Smith:**
Ad Hoc Governments
11. **Ronald Gallimore, Joan Whitehorn Boggs, and Cathie Jordan:**
Culture, Behavior and Education
12. **Howard W. Hallman:**
Neighborhood Government in a Metropolitan Setting
13. **Richard J. Gelles:**
The Violent Home
14. **Jerry L. Weaver:**
Conflict and Control in Health Care Administration
15. **Gebhard Ludwig Schweigler:**
National Consciousness in Divided Germany
16. **James T. Carey:**
Sociology and Public Affairs
17. **Edward W. Lehman:**
Coordinating Health Care
18. **Charles G. Bell and Charles M. Price:**
The First Term
19. **Clayton P. Alderfer and L. Dave Brown:**
Learning from Changing
20. **L. Edward Wells and Gerald Marwell:**
Self-Esteem
21. **Robert S. Robins:**
Political Institutionalization and the Integration of Elites
22. **William R. Schonfeld:**
Obedience and Revolt
23. **William C. McCready and Andrew M. Greeley:**
The Ultimate Values of the American Population
24. **F. Ivan Nye:**
Role Structure and Analysis of the Family
25. **Paul Wehr and Michael Washburn:**
Peace and World Order Systems
26. **Patricia R. Stewart:**
Children in Distress
27. **Juergen Dedring:**
Recent Advances in Peace and Conflict Research
28. **Moshe M. Czudnowski:**
Comparing Political Behavior
29. **Jack D. Douglas:**
Investigative Social Research
30. **Michael Stohl:**
War and Domestic Political Violence
31. **Nancy E. Williamson:**
Sons or Daughters
32. **Werner Levi:**
Law and Politics in the International Society
33. **David L. Altheide:**
Creating Reality
34. **Allan Lerner:**
The Politics of Decision-Making
35. **Philip E. Converse:**
The Dynamics of Party Support
36. **Charles L. Newman and Barbara R. Price:**
Jails and Drug Treatment
37. **Clarence L. Abercrombie III:**
The Military Chaplain
38. **Mark Gottdiener:**
Planned Sprawl
39. **Robert L. Lineberry:**
Equality and Urban Policy
40. **Patrick M. Morgan:**
Deterrence
41. **Vladimir A. Lefebvre:**
The Structure of Awareness
42. **Andrea Fontana:**
The Last Frontier
43. **Robert V. Kemper:**
Migration and Adaptation
44. **David Caplovitz and Fred Sherrow:**
The Religious Drop-Outs
45. **Stuart S. Nagel and Marian Neef:**
The Legal Process: Modeling the System
46. **Rue Bucher and Joan G. Stelling:**
Becoming Professional
47. **Paul Hiniker:**
Revolutionary Ideology and Chinese Reality
48. **Simon N. Herman:**
Jewish Identity
49. **Alan Marsh:**
Protest and Political Consciousness
50. **Ralph LaRossa:**
Conflict and Power in Marriage
51. **Bengt Abrahamsson:**
Bureaucracy or Participation
52. **F. Parkinson:**
The Philosophy of International Relations

301.58
C244r
BV
4531.2
.C33
1977

THE RELIGIOUS DROP-OUTS

APOSTASY AMONG COLLEGE GRADUATES

DAVID CAPLOVITZ
FRED SHERROW

With the assistance of
STANLEY RAFFEL and STEVEN COHEN

Volume 44
SAGE LIBRARY OF
SOCIAL RESEARCH

SAGE PUBLICATIONS Beverly Hills London

24594

Copyright © 1977 by Sage Publications, Inc.

All rights reserved. No part of this book may be reproduced or utilized in any form or by any means, electronic or mechanical, including photocopying, recording, or by any information storage and retrieval system, without permission in writing from the publisher.

For information address:

SAGE PUBLICATIONS, INC.
275 South Beverly Drive
Beverly Hills, California 90212

SAGE PUBLICATIONS LTD
28 Banner Street
London EC1Y 8QE

Printed in the United States of America

Library of Congress Cataloging in Publication Data

Caplovitz, David.
The religious drop-outs

(Sage library of social research ; v. 44)
Includes index.
1. College students–United States–Religious life. 2. Apostasy. I. Sherrow, Fred, joint author. II. Title.
BV4531.2.C33 301.5'8 77-1043
ISBN 0-8039-0714-1
ISBN 0-8039-0715-X pbk.

FIRST PRINTING

CONTENTS

To Our Parents

Jennie and Harry Caplovitz

and

Celia and Benjamin Sherrow

IN MEMORIAM

Fred Sherrow, the coauthor of this book, died of cancer on November 26, 1971, at the age of 31. Fred Sherrow was my student, my colleague, and my close friend, especially during the years 1965 through 1971 when he was a graduate student at Columbia. Fred was a student in the first college course that I, a freshly minted Ph.D., ever taught, a course on methodology at Columbia College in the fall of 1961. Fred, who was then a senior in the college, became forever etched in my brain because of an absurd incident in the life of a novice teacher. During the first weeks of the course, I had the students, whose names I hardly knew, hand in a small assignment. One of these papers was brilliant, but to my chagrin, on the day I handed back the papers, the author of the brilliant paper was absent. When the class was over, I saw in the hall Fred Sherrow, who was absent from the class that day, and I rushed up to him and said, "Are you Goldman?" (the author of the brilliant paper). When he answered "No," I could hardly disguise my disappointment and I blurted out, "Who is Goldman?" Fred Sherrow looked at me and replied, "Who indeed is Goldman?"

One of the rare rewards of being a teacher is the opportunity to influence the lives of students, and Fred Sherrow became a source of immense gratification for me because of the circumstances that allowed me to influence his life. In 1964 I returned to Columbia to head a graduate training program after a two year sojurn at the University of Chicago. One day, during my first year back, I was having a drink with a friend in the West

End Bar when, through the window, I saw Fred Sherrow walk by. I raced out of the West End and invited him to join us. I learned that he had spent some time in Israel and was determined to settle there. He was about to embark on a course of study at Columbia's Teachers College because he believed that a degree in education would qualify him for employment in Israel. My friend and I tried to convince him to do graduate work in sociology instead. We urged him to talk to Professor Paul Lazarsfeld, who was then advising various Israeli universities on how to develop research institutes. Lazarsfeld somehow managed to persuade Fred to become a graduate student in sociology, and he enrolled in the department in the fall of 1965, assisted by a fellowship in my program. As one of my trainees, Fred had to take my course in quantitative analysis, and the paper that he wrote in that course evolved into the present study of apostasy.

The apostasy study, funded by a grant from the American Jewish Committee, and a totally different study, an evaluation of an Israeli work-study program for American college students known as Sherut La'am, a study financed by the Jewish Agency, led to Fred's moving from my student to my colleague. I would never have taken on either of these studies if I could not have counted on Fred Sherrow to do the lion's share of the work. From student to colleague, Fred Sherrow soon became a close friend. There is something extraordinarily exhiliarating about working with another person on an intellectual enterprise that happens to be funded research and requires meeting deadlines. The exchange of ideas, the sharing of the work, and the evolution of a joint product that meets one's inner standards of competence, in addition to meeting a deadline, is incredibly rewarding and leads to a close bond with the partner in the enterprise. Through this bond, Fred became a dear friend. During my relationship with Fred, I was exposed to only a few facets of this complicated man. I knew him as an intellectual and researcher, as an extremely hard-working, thorough, and creative analyst of data. Fred and I also shared another life. We were both in love with New York's professional sports teams.

We cheered and mourned over the fortunes of the Knicks, the Mets, the Giants, the Jets, the Rangers, and even the Yankees.

I intuitively knew that there was another Fred, a Fred with a deep commitment to the Jewish religion, the Jewish community, and the state of Israel, but because my interests in these topics did not run as deep as his, I did not come to know and appreciate the full depth of Fred's commitment to Judaism until after his death. But there is one anecdote revealing Fred's Jewish commitment that I will always cherish. When we applied to the American Jewish Committee for money for the apostasy study, we were invited to lunch at the committee where we were closely interviewed by five or six senior members of the AJC staff. The lunch took place in the AJC dining room. From the tone of the questions addressed to us it became clear that one of the major fears of the AJC representatives was that our research might in some unwitting way reflect negatively upon the Jews. As this discussion took place, lunch was served. Lunch consisted of cheeseburgers and milk. Only one of the seven or eight people present did not eat lunch that day: Fred Sherrow. When I understood the gist of the concern of the AJC representatives, I called their attention to Fred's abstinence and said, "Surely you don't think that my research team would do anything to harm the Jews." Fred's abstinence did as much as anything to insure the grant that made the apostasy study possible.

At a memorial service for Fred, I heard the rabbi of Columbia University humbly explain that Fred has been his teacher and had helped him to adjust to his job at Columbia. I soon learned that Fred Sherrow had almost singlehandedly organized the Columbia Jewish community, from Friday night services to Monday night Israeli dances, to the issue of Soviet Jewry, to the founding of a campus newspaper, the Jewish Free Press, which was distributed at colleges throughout the city. Shortly after Fred's death, the students at Columbia rented a brownstone from Columbia and opened a Jewish communal residence and activity center which they named after him, *Beit Ephraim* (Fred's House).

In the very long time that it has taken me to bring this joint enterprise to completion (nine years), I have been driven by a compulsion to have Fred's work published so that a much wider world might know about this extraordinary man. With the publication of this book, an enormous burden has been lifted from my shoulders.

New York *David Caplovitz*

FOREWORD

Cast your bread on the waters, for at long last you will recover it.

Ecclesiastes 11:1

It happened so long ago. Was the menu really as David Caplovitz remembers it in his "In Memoriam"?

Professor Caplovitz is an eminent practitioner of quantitative social research. He and his colleagues cannot be entirely happy with their lot. In the British usage, they are numerate. (Numerate is to numbers as literate is to letters.) If we were illiterate we would be ashamed. Since we are only innumerate, we make a virtue of our vice. In our own eyes we are qualitative, fine. They, the numerate and quantitative, are coarse.

In this instance, at least, let us acknowledge our debt. Having to rely on information gathered by others, for other purposes, Caplovitz and Sherrow nevertheless teach us much that we need to know about religion and community in the United States, and perhaps in other countries too.

The time is the 1960s and their aftermath. From one point of view, those years continue the history of the decline of religion that started with science and the Enlightenment. Our twentieth-century *Entzauberung der Welt,* "the world's dis-enchantment," echoes Schiller's eighteenth-century "Nature bereft of gods."

From another point of view, the 60s were also the time of the Counterculture. In France revolutionary students called for "all power to imagination!" At MIT, the very citadel of science, Huston Smith has reported that some of his best students would make no important decision without first consulting *I Ching.* Antiwar demonstrators could think to levitate the Pentagon by means of a Tibetan rite of exorcism. When boy met girl they would exchange not only their names but also their signs of the zodiac (Margaret Mead not wholly disapproving). They still do. As this book notes, exotic cults still abound.

It can be argued, therefore, that what is striking about the educated young today is not the old decline of the old religions but the new decline of science and rise of superstition—not Psalms' "the fool says in his heart, 'There is no God' " (14:1 and 53:2[1]) but Deuteronomy's "they sacrificed to demons, no-gods, gods they had never known, new ones, come lately" (32:17).

For Professor Caplovitz it is the intellectuals who, having "most acutely experienced the clash between fundamental religious doctrine and the ideas of modern science," are "committed to rationality and empiricism." That seems to be true of nuclear physicists and molecular biologists, or most of them—the scientific intellectuals. Is it true of other intellectuals? Since Romanticism the poets and literary intellectuals have been more alienated and rebellious, whether leftward or rightward, than the scientists. The premier intellectual, rebel, and apostate of our day is Sartre. No one has ever accused Sartre of empiricism or science.

For Catholic apostasy, I am unsure about the weight we should give to upward mobility. Is the mobility a fact? Then maybe it is as much the effect as the cause of apostasy, or maybe both are caused or favored by some third fact—e.g., assimilation. (Distinguishing between fact and ideology, a Jew of old French stock has said of himself and others like him that they are no longer assimilationist, they are merely assimilated.) Or is the mobility an ambition? Then one would expect the example of Kennedy's presidency to have weakened rather than strengthened Catholic apostasy for ambition's sake.

Among Jews a saying attributed to Heinrich Heine has long been popular: *wie es sich christelt, so jüdelt es sich,* "as the Christians do, so do the Jews." That is not confirmed in this book. At the beginning of the 60s proportionately more Jews were leaving their communion and community than Protestants and especially Catholics. In the 20s and 30s, as Nathan Glazer records in *American Judaism,* the difference had been even more pronounced. By the end of the 60s the Jewish rate was slowing down while the Christian ones were speeding up. That Jews more than Christians kept going back to what they had once left behind was not new. *Commentary* published Chandler Brossard's "Plaint of a Gentile Intellectual" in 1950–the plaint being that "you can't go home again" applied pretty stringently to Gentile intellectuals, while Jewish intellectuals appeared able to go home again as often as they liked.

Caplovitz rightly associates universalism with apostasy. In 1919 Veblen had already judged universalist apostasy to be a necessary condition for the "Intellectual Preeminence of Jews in Modern Europe." But the 60s were lean years for universalism. They were the time of Scottish, Welsh, Breton, Basque, and Palestinian nationalisms, of Black Power (and Red, and Brown), of the New Ethnicity, of Affirmative Action.

For Jews the 60s also witnessed the Six-day War and Soviet Jewry's dry bones living again. These could almost tempt the most positivist ("empirical") to imagine they were in the presence of something numinous–though they would have been too bashful or actually ashamed to admit it, to themselves no less than to others.

In Judaism the religious and the secular, like the religious and the ethnic, so-called, have never been sharply set off from each other. As with the assimilationism and assimilation of Jews, so with their secularism and secularity. It is the ideology that is in retreat.

There is a Yiddish expression, "it's hard to be a Jew." This can mean that God has imposed more commandments upon the Jews than upon others. Or it can invoke persecution, and worse. Usually it has meant that in the climb to success, Jews have more obstacles to overcome than others. As late as 1963 a president of the American Historical Association could publicly regret the "products of lower-middle-class or foreign origins" in his profession. For some this called to mind the German principle, not renounced even in the Weimar Republic, that Jews were too *wesenfremd,* alien from the folk essence, to teach German history or literature. No wonder that, without being careerist, Jews who yearned for an academic or intellectual career should have tried to make themselves acceptable by apostasy. Apostasy had two advantages. It was at once less drastic and more honorable than the expedient baptism of a Heine, and surely an apostate Jew was less *wesenfremd* than the other kind.

By the end of the 60s apostasy could more easily be dispensed with. The cost of Jewish affirmation had come down.

For this, as for much else, see S.M. Lipset and E.C. Ladd, Jr., "Jewish Academics in the United States," *American Jewish Year Book,* 1971.

It remains only to lament again Fred Sherrow, who died untimely, and to thank again David Caplovitz, who has written this book to serve as instruction for us and as a pious memorial of his student, colleague, and friend.

May 1977
The American Jewish Committee *Milton Himmelfarb*

PREFACE

All too frequently, research monographs are presented to an unsuspecting world as if their authors had in mind from the outset the final form of their work. I am convinced that an important obligation of the researcher is to report not only his finished product, but the fits and starts, the twists and turns that led to the final result and, for this reason, I take the opportunity to reconstruct the history of this study. The need for such an accounting is all the more pressing in the present instance because of the inordinate time that has passed from the inception to the conclusion of this project. Almost ten years have gone by since we first received a grant from the American Jewish Committee in the spring of 1966 to carry out a study of Jewish identity. How a modest study evolved into the present monograph, how the work was done, how the roles were divided between the various collaborators, and why it took so long to carry out this assignment are the main topics dealt with here. In passing, we shall also document some intellectual history, the invention and diffusion of a new research tool that made this study possible.

NORC and the Emergence of a New Research Tradition

Ever since survey research came into being as a major tool of social science, it has been standard procedure to collect information on "background" variables, the data that permit locating respondents in the social structure. Thus, hardly a survey is done without questions on age, sex, income, occupation, education and, frequently, religion. An innovation in this standard package occurred in 1956 when, in a study of the financing of graduate education carried out by the National Opinion Research Center of the University of Chicago, a second religious question was included. The respondent was asked to state in which religion he had been raised as well as what his current religion was. In devising both questions, the NORC research team gave formal recognition to the dynamic nature of religious affiliation, thereby converting what most researchers had perceived as an ascribed, unchanging characteristic to one that has elements of achievement as well. As a result of these two questions, it became possible for the first time to identify converts and apostates, that is, those who had left their religion of origin for some other religion or for no religion. The director of the NORC study in which this invention occurred was James Davis, and I am most happy to acknowledge him as the inventor of the two religious questions.[1] The problem is that Jim denies that this was his invention and gives credit to unknown members of his research staff. I have approached both Joseph Spaeth and Joseph Zelan, who assisted Jim in this study, but neither one of them claims authorship of the invention and thus, in the absence of more precise information, I gratefully credit the research team of *Stipends and Spouses* for this addition to survey research.

The NORC team was quick to seize upon the implications of their invention. Joseph Zelan was the first to carry out a statistical analysis of apostasy, initially as a master's essay in the sociology department of the University of Chicago and later as a journal article.[2] The Zelan analysis was based on the 1956 data on graduate students. In 1961, NORC launched a massive panel study of college graduates of that year. The purpose was to examine the dynamics of occupational choice and career development. NORC routinely included the two religion questions in the research instrument of the study, and Andrew Greeley based his dissertation dealing with religion and career choice on these data, devoting a full chapter to apostasy.[3]

As is true of all good inventions, this one quickly diffused to other research centers. Commencing in 1966, the American Council on Education included the two religion questions in its annual surveys of incoming college freshmen, a tradition that was carried on in the Carnegie study of higher education in 1969 when the two questions appeared on the questionnaires administered to undergraduates, graduates, and faculty members.[4]

In 1964, I returned to Columbia after two years at the University of Chicago and the National Opinion Research Center, and I became a carrier of the two religion questions. An undergraduate student at Columbia, Harry Levy, did a senior thesis under my direction in the spring of 1965 based on a survey of interreligious dating among Columbia and Barnard students. I insisted that he include the two religion questions in his questionnaire, which was answered by 380 Columbia and Barnard undergraduates, and I collaborated with him on a report on interreligious dating.[5]

The Origins of the Apostasy Study

In the fall of 1965, I found the Levy survey a useful tool for teaching my students the art of survey analysis. Each student was required to write a paper based on the Levy data. Fred Sherrow chose to write about those respondents who had been raised as Jews but no longer adhered to any religion. His paper, which he conceived of as a study of Jewish identity, was first rate and became the genesis of the present book. Some time after the Sherrow paper was completed, he approached me with the idea of obtaining the data from the NORC 1961 panel study of college graduates and doing a more detailed analysis of Jewish identity. I welcomed the idea and contacted my friends at NORC to find out how much it would cost to obtain the data. I then called a friend who was working in the research department of the American Jewish Committee and sounded him out about the possibilities of a grant from the committee to make this study possible. Soon I submitted a proposal to the

AJC, which they graciously funded. Their funds made it possible to buy the NORC data and to pay Fred Sherrow's summer salary and the salary of another student who joined the team, Stanley Raffel.

One dilemma of the research team assembled to write a report on Jewish identity was that each of its members had other obligations. I was fully committed to several funded research projects that I was directing. Both Fred and Stanley were busy taking courses and writing papers for their course work, and the advanced graduate student who had approached me together with Fred with the idea of getting the NORC data was fully involved in his dissertation. During the first year of the project, the great bulk of the work was done by Fred and Stanley. As the leader, I quickly evolved a table of organization of the chapters, one that served reasonably well through the life of the project. According to an early memorandum prepared in the fall of 1966, I envisioned nine data chapters, following an introductory chapter:

Chapter 2:	Social Origins and Apostasy
Chapter 3:	Personality, Value-Orientations and Apostasy
Chapter 4:	School Experiences and Apostasy
Chapter 5:	Career Choice and Apostasy
Chapter 6:	The College Context of Apostasy
Chapter 7:	The Dynamics of Apostasy
Chapter 8:	Intermarriage and Its Resolution
Chapter 9:	The Correlates of Intermarriage
Chapter 10:	Apostasy and Intermarriage Among the Christians

Since this is a history of a research project written with the intention of sharing knowledge with other researchers with the goal of making research more manageable and improving its quality, perhaps a digression is in order. I am convinced that the most important research act is evolving a table of contents of the final report before a single piece of data analysis is carried out. The tragic mistake committed over and over again by amateur researchers, typically graduate students, is the practice of having the computer, which can spit out countless numbers of tables in a minute or two, run every variable against every other variable. This approach to research is best characterized as *crass empiricism*,[6] a disease that affects graduate students in particular, but even more advanced social scientists as well. The adherents of crass empiricism believe that if only they run enough tables and examine the computer-generated tests of significance, they will be able to write a report or dissertation. Crass empiricists are easy to recognize, for their offices are filled with pounds of computer output. Among other flaws, crass empiricism fails to take into account that, by chance alone, five out of every hundred tables will achieve an acceptable level of significance. The antidote to crass empiricism, the mark of the good researcher, is, of course, having a *reason* for running a table, that is, having an expectation that variable A will be related to variable B. Once such an expectation can be justified, the outcome of the table is irrelevant. Either the table supports the expectation, which is a tribute to the theoretical reasoning of the analyst, or the expected relationship does not occur, which is an equally valuable contribution to science, reminiscent of Robert Oppenheimer's explanation of his excitement after a seminar at the Center for Advanced Studies, namely that everything they thought was true was false. The table may have yet a third outcome, the relationship between A and B may be the opposite of the expected one. This should be the cause of even more excitement. Such joys of research are never shared by the crass empiricist, for he proceeds without any expectations at all in the false hope that the computer will tell him something he has not thought of. Crass empiricism is much more of a danger today because of the ease with which computers generate tables. In the days of the counter sorter, it was hard work to be a crass empiricist, even if one was so inclined, because of the labor involved. To impress my students with the evils of crass empiricism and to provide them with a guide for avoiding this sin, I have suggested to them a formula for judging their excellence as researchers. This consists of the ratio of tables in the final report to pounds of computer output. I have suggested that if their research efforts yield a whole number for this calculation, they are ahead of the game.

The best antidote to crass empiricism is to work out the organizational scheme of the final report before looking at any tables. This intellectual task demonstrates, more than anything else, the researcher's command of his project. One might well ask where tables of content come from. The answer is that they stem from the need to tell a story about a phenomenon in much the same way as a historian or reporter would do it. A very common organizational scheme is a chronological one, and, as can be seen, the apostasy story line is so based. The first analytical chapter deals with social origins, the next with personality and values presumably developed during the formative years of adolescence. This is followed by a chapter on the college experience, which in turn is followed by one on careers, which postdate college. The chronological line is interrupted to consider a contextual variable, the college attended, and is then resumed with the issue of the dynamics of apostasy based on the data collected three years later. Finally, we consider the issue of intermarriage, which is also based on data from the later survey, and which chronologically tends to follow the college experience. It is important to note that usually more than one organizational scheme can be justified, and that different analysts will approach the same material from different perspectives. In the present instance, some justification could be made for beginning the story with the dynamics of apostasy, identifying the confirmed identifiers, the confirmed apostates, and the two groups of changers, and then devoting the entire analysis to an explication of these four types of students. So much for the digression on data analysis.

Fred Sherrow went to work on drafts of the social-origin chapter, the chapter on school experiences and on career choice. Stanley Raffel did the first draft of the personality-value-orientation chapter and, during the second year, he worked on the chapter reporting apostasy and intermarriage among Protestants and Catholics, and Fred did the first drafts of the two chapters dealing with intermarriage.

It should be noted that we promised the American Jewish Committee that we would complete a report on Jewish identity within a year or two, and, in fact, in the spring of 1967, on the basis of the work done by Fred and Stanley, I prepared a forty-page report which so pleased the American Jewish Committee that they issued a press release, and accounts of this research appeared in papers throughout the country in June of 1967. For all intents and purposes, we had fulfilled our obligation to the committee with this report. But the considerable work invested by Fred and Stanley made us realize that we had the makings of a book, and we were determined to plunge on.

One part of the outline presented above quickly fell apart, the two chapters dealing with college experiences and career choices. The original draft of the college-experience chapter related apostasy to undergraduate major, grades, and organizational activities, and it soon became clear that an underlying theme of this chapter was the student's commitment to an intellectual way of life. Thus, students majoring in the humanities or sciences were more likely to apostatize than those majoring in business or education, and those who worked on college newspapers and literary magazines were more likely to apostatize than those who did not engage in such activities. The chapter that Fred Sherrow wrote on career choice and apostasy proved to be rather repetitious. Thus, those electing to go to graduate school were more likely to apostatize than those opting for professional school or for no further education, and those opting for careers in the natural and social sciences or humanities were more likely to apostatize than those oriented toward professional, educational, or business careers. The realization of this repetition led us to conclude, in the winter of 1967, that these chapters should be abandoned and replaced by a single chapter relating intellectualism to apostasy. About this time, I also became aware that religiosity, initially conceived as one of the personality traits to be examined in Chapter 3, deserved to be a chapter in its own right, a chapter that would examine the interaction of religiosity and the other germs of apostasy in the generation of apostasy. Hence, the origin of what is now Chapter 5.

The initial organizational scheme became modified in two other respects. By 1968-1969, Fred Sherrow had completed his course requirements and examinations and needed a dissertation topic. He and I agreed that he should write his dissertation on intermarriage, and the idea of two companion volumes, one on apostasy and one on intermarriage, evolved. Once this decision was made, the two chapters dealing with intermarriage (Chapter 8 and 9 in the above scheme), the first drafts of which were written by Fred and the subsequent ones by me, were taken out of the apostasy book and relegated to Fred's dissertation.

In June of 1968, Stanley Raffel completed a draft of the last data chapter, the one dealing with apostasy and intermarriage among Protestants and Catholics. I read Stanley's draft and became sick. Stanley's tables showed that all the findings pertaining to Jews presented in the earlier chapters held for Protestants and Catholics as well. The flaw in the original table of organization was evident from the language that Stanley had to use to describe the findings. Each table he presented was introduced by a sentence like, "Just as we saw in Chapter X, so we now see that . . . ." With sickening heart, I realized that my organizational scheme was wrong and that the Protestants and Catholics had to be given parity with the Jews. By this time, more or less final drafts, that is, chapters that I had rewritten, existed for social origins, personality traits and value orientations, religiosity, the college context, intermarriage, and the consequences of intermarriage. In July of 1968, I announced to my colleagues my discovery and pointed out to them that we were no longer in the Jewish-identity business but rather in the business of religious apostasy and religious intermarriage whatever the religion.[7] Fred, Stanley, and, in particular, the advanced graduate student, were rather upset by my announcement, but I assured them that it would not take much work to revise the chapters and give equity to the Christians. One reason that this seemed at first a difficult task was that it meant presenting our findings in three parts rather than one. Instead of showing how two variables were related among Jews, we had to repeat this analysis for Protestants and Catholics within each table. During late July and all of August of 1968, I reworked the chapters on hand, giving the Protestants and Catholics equality with the Jews, and by September rather complete versions existed of the following chapters: social origins, personality and value-orientations, religiosity, the college context, intermarriage and the correlates of intermarriage. In addition, a good draft of the introductory chapter existed. In fact, at that time, before Fred Sherrow's dissertation on intermarriage was formulated, two years after the project started, and eight years ago as this is written, all but two of the data chapters then envisioned existed in more or less final form. How, then, was it possible that eight more years had to pass before the book was completed?[8] The answer is that I had to leave apostasy and pay attention to my main responsibilities, the care of large-scale funded projects that were paying my salary. By January of 1969, the data that I had assembled for a large study of breakdowns in consumer-credit transactions were ready for analysis, and I naively assumed that I could complete that report in six months or so and then return to apostasy. In fact, it took two and a half years of more or less full-time work to complete the debtor study and an additional half year or more to revise the report for publication.[9]

Still another responsibility that became due during this time was a survey of businessmen in Harlem, which I had volunteered to supervise on behalf of a group concerned with the development of black capitalism. This meant taking a few months from the debtor study to complete the businessmen report.[10]

During the spring and summer of 1969, Fred Sherrow wrote extensive drafts of the two missing chapters, the one on intellectualism and the one of the dynamics of apostasy. I was too busy during 1969, 1970, and 1971 with my consumer study to even read Fred's drafts. In fact, it was not until some months after his death that I read the chapters, and I then experienced a most eerie feeling. I wanted to reach for the phone and congratulate him on some analytical decision or question him about another, and it was quite a start to realize that the voice I was hearing was dead. These chapters were not fully revised by me until the fall of 1972 and the spring of 1973, more than a year after Fred's death.

When the consumer-debtor study was completed, other professional activities occupied my time, and it was not until the summer of 1974 that I was able to clear the decks and make a concerted effort to complete the apostasy study. By this time, the apostasy manuscript had acquired a serious flaw: The data were quite old. I knew that I had to find more recent data if the book was to achieve the credibility that it deserved. Fortunately, the large-scale Carnegie study of higher education carried out in 1969, which incorporated the two NORC religion questions, was available, as was an additional wave of the NORC panel study administered to a subsample of the class of 1961 in 1968, and the annual surveys of entering freshmen conducted by the American Council on Education. These materials provided the basis for Chapter 8 of this book. To prove the old adage that every dark cloud has a silver lining, the inordinate delay in completing this book is in part justified by the new materials presented in Chapter 8, for they shed further light on the processes and trends in apostasy among college graduates.

The role of Stanley Raffel has already been explained. As the author of first drafts of two of the chapters, one of which survived, there is some justification for Stanley's being listed as an author. Stanley himself, however, has felt that his contribution did not warrant authorship, and he prefers the present form of acknowledgement to him. Remaining to be explained is the role of Steven Cohen. Steven was Fred Sherrow's roommate. At the time of Fred's death, Steven was in his first year of graduate school in sociology at Columbia. Steven stepped into Fred's shoes in many ways. He provided me with all the tables that I needed to revise old chapters and work on new ones. In addition, he did the regression analysis of the determinants of apostasy referred to in the concluding chapter. And, like Fred before him, Steven Cohen became my close friend. Steven stepped into Fred's shoes in yet another respect: He became the leader of the Jewish community at Columbia. It was Steven Cohen who organized and became the first President of Beit Ephraim, the Jewish commune at Columbia named after Fred Sherrow.

The foregoing may sound like a confession, but it is really intended to perform what I consider to be a most important function: informing the consumers of empirical research about the facts of the production of the product. The history of this study exemplifies the discoveries and pressures that resulted in the revision and evolution of well-intentioned research plans. I am convinced, as is my mentor, Paul Lazarsfeld, that through such histories of the various phases of research projects, the cause of methodology will be fruitfully advanced. My hope is that other researchers will take heart from this "confession" and tell it like it really is so that we may all learn.

New York *David Caplovitz*

NOTES

1. See James A. Davis, *Stipends and Spouses,* Chicago: University of Chicago Press, 1962.

2. Joseph Zelan, "Correlates of Religious Apostasy," unpublished Master's essay, University of Chicago, 1960; and Zelan, "Religious Apostasy, Higher Education and Occupational Choice," *Sociology of Education,* Vol. 41, No. 4, Fall, 1968.

3. Andrew Greeley, *Religion and Career,* New York: Sheed and Ward, 1963.

4. The undergraduates in the Carnegie study were sampled from the lists of entering freshmen who had completed ACE questionnaires at the beginning of their college careers, making the undergraduate part of the Carnegie study into a panel study. For the undergraduates, information on religion of origin was obtained when they started college, and the Carnegie undergraduate questionnaire, unlike the questionnaire used in the graduate-student and faculty surveys, inquired only about current religion.

5. See David Caplovitz and Harry Levy, *Interreligious Dating Among College Students,* Bureau of Applied Social Research, Columbia University, 1965. I became the senior author when Harry, having graduated from Columbia college, chose to vacation in Greece during the summer of 1965, rather than write the report.

6. I first heard this phrase used by Robert Merton in a lecture many years ago at Columbia.

7. The only remnant from the earlier definition of our research problem is that the Jews are listed first in all the tables presented in this book.

8. The manuscript was completed in early 1967, but a contract for its publication was not signed until a year and a half later.

9. David Caplovitz, *Consumers in Trouble: A Study of Debtors in Default,* New York: Free Press, 1974. One reason for my miscalculation of how long it would take to complete the debtor study was that, during the data-processing phase of the study, I was so absorbed in apostasy that I allowed my research assistants to make major data-processing decisions. When I returned to the debtor study in January of 1969, I discovered a major data-processing error and, instead of writing a report, I spent the first four months recoding the data. At the risk of boring the lay reader, I would like to tell the students of methodology and research who read this what the serious coding error was. A major theme of the debtor study was to describe why the relationship had broken down, that is, why the debtor had stopped paying. From the outset of the project, I assumed that the reasons fell into two major categories, inability to pay and refusal to pay because of defective merchandise or fraud on the part of the seller. When I returned to the project in January of 1969 and examined the codebook, I discovered, to my dismay, that my coders had placed almost 40 percent of the reasons for default into a mysterious "other" category. It was this discovery that led me to recode "reasons" on all the questionnaires into a classificatory scheme consisting of more than 50 categories. The results of this work can be seen in *Consumers in Trouble.* Instead of one chapter dealing with reasons for default, there are six.

10. David Caplovitz, *The Merchants of Harlem: A Study of Small Business in a Black Community,* Beverly Hills: Sage, 1973.

Chapter 1

INTRODUCTION

The past hundred years have witnessed a great decline in the authority of religion in the daily affairs of Western society. The sphere of religion has been sharply segregated from other institutional spheres. And yet, in spite of the process of secularization, religion and religious communities still remain vital forces, even in the most complex of modern societies—the United States. Most Americans still retain a religious identification and consider themselves part of one of the three major religious communities in America, Protestantism, Catholicism, and Judaism. The most recent surveys indicate that 94 percent of Americans identify with some religious group and that 94 percent also believe in God.[1]

These signs of the vitality of religion in modern society notwithstanding, there has been much concern in religious circles about the relevance of religion to modern life. The "God-is-dead" thesis in Protestant circles symbolizes the soul-searching on the part of Protestant theologians as to the relevance of religious doctrine to modern life. The major reforms initiated by the Vatican council are also symptomatic of the effort to make the Roman Catholic church more meaningful to its constituents. For the Jewish community, the problem of adaptation to modern conditions is even more complicated. Judaism represents not only a religion for many but, for perhaps even more, a kind of ethnic identity. Assimilationist forces at work in America have led to a deep concern among leaders of the Jewish community about the problem of sustaining a Jewish identity (of which religion is one component) in the younger generations of American Jews. The oldest generation, socialized in the ghettos of Europe, is dying out, and the problem of retaining the loyalties of the younger generations raised in the relative freedom of America is one of grave concern to the Jewish community.

To assess the future of America's religious communities, it is necessary to examine today's younger generations, for they in particular are exposed to the secularizing forces at work in modern society. This is especially the case for the college-educated among younger Americans. If, several generations ago, it was quite an achievement to win a high school diploma, it is more and more true today that success depends on a college diploma. Each year, the number of college graduates increases, and it is this group that is most apt to experience conflicts between religious and secular forces. After all, religion has been undermined by the development of science, and higher education not only fosters scientific development, but imparts this knowledge to its constituents. The growth of science—of rational interpretations of the world based on empirical evidence—is at the heart of the process of rationalization that Weber wrote about and has been the major force restricting the nonempirical religious view of the world.

The potential strain between higher education and religiosity has been widely recognized and has attracted the attention of scholars. There is now a rather extensive literature on the degree of religiosity among college students. A study in the early sixties by Goldsen et al.[2] found that most college students felt a need for religious belief and believe in some version of God. And yet the authors concluded that religiosity among college students tended to be secular in nature. Students generally held quite liberal, rather than orthodox, fundamentalistic views of religion. The study also showed that the self-reported religiosity of students had little bearing on the moral decisions of their day-to-day lives. Upon closer examination, the researchers found that more than half of those who reported a need for religion were referring to some "sincere working philosophy or code of ethics" and not necessarily to religious belief.[3]

In a review of many studies of religion among college students, Clyde Parker has shown that most of the research tends to confirm the findings of Goldsen et al.[4] The studies generally find that most college students in the United States claim to have some religious belief, but that their beliefs tend to be liberal rather than fundamentalistic. Only a minority believe in a personal God who intervenes in the affairs of individuals or in life after death. Parker's review of the evidence finds that there is considerable variation in kinds of religious belief between students in colleges located in different sections of the country (the Northeastern colleges being associated with liberal religious veiws and Southern colleges with fundamentalistic views), between the sexes (women having stronger religious commitments than men), and among the three major religions (Catholic students demonstrating the most religiosity, Jewish students the least, with Protestants in between.)[5]

This monograph is intended as another contribution to this tradition of research. It too deals with that segment of the population most susceptible to the strains placed on religious identification, young college graduates. But it differs from the previous studies in placing emphasis not upon religiosity but upon identification with a religious group. Lenski and Herberg and others (including Goldsen et al.) have pointed out that a religious identity is based not only upon religious belief, but also upon a sense of communality. According to this thesis, the major religions in America operate as comprehensive ethnic groups toward which the members experience a sense of group loyalty and from which, as in other social groups, they acquire many of their value-orientations and attitudes. The extent to which religious belief is essential to a religious identification is an empirical question. As we shall soon see, its importance varies from one religion to another.

The data for this research come from an extensive panel study of occupational choice of college students carried out by the National Opinion Research Center. Over a three year period, beginning in 1961, NORC administered yearly questionnaires to a large sample of college graduates–33,782 of whom first completed a questionnaire toward the end of their senior year in college.[6] Unlike the usual survey that includes among the standard package of background questions a question about current religious affiliation, this one also asked what religion the respondent was raised in. Thus, for the second time in any large-scale national survey, it became possible to identify individuals who no longer adhered to the religion of their parents.[7] Since the NORC survey was not designed as a study of religious identity, there are, of course, many gaps in the available data. Strictly speaking, we have information on religious identification, that is, whether one claims to belong to a religious group, and its obverse, the abandonment of such an identification, a phenomenon only poorly captured by the term "apostasy." According to Webster's dictionary, "apostasy" refers to the abandonment of a set of principles or faith, *not* the replacement of one set of principles by another. Thus, we use the term "apostasy" to refer to students who report having been raised in a particular religion but at the time they were filling out the questionnaire, adhered to *no* religion. This definition excludes those who converted to some other religion.[8] The subsequent analysis thus deals with apostates and those who continued to adhere to the religion in which they were raised, the identifiers.

The Meaning and Extent of Apostasy

In the strict sense, apostasy means the relinquishing of a set of religious beliefs. But it can be argued, especially for Jews and to some extent for Protestants and Catholics as well, that identification with a religion has an element of group identification independent of religious belief. Much has been written about what it is to be a Jew, particularly in the American context, and the extent to which religious belief is essential to Jewishness. People who define themselves as Jews and are so defined by others, but are not at all religious, are quite common. Religiosity is clearly only one component and not an essential one for Jewish identification. To a lesser degree, the same may be said of those raised as Protestants or Catholics. Some Catholics and Protestants who do not consider themselves religious, who do not attend religious services, and who have serious questions about doctrinal matters, do not hesitate to identify themselves as Catholics or Protestants. For them, "religion" is more a basis of communality than of a commitment to a particular ideology. A central thesis of this book is that apostasy indicates not only loss of religious faith, but rejection of a particular ascriptive community as a basis for self-identification.

The chief objective of this monograph will be to discover the determinants of apostasy among American college graduates. As a prelude to this task, we present the facts about apostasy in this population of college seniors. But first, a methodological note is in order. The NORC study deliberately oversampled large colleges and weights were assigned to make the sample representative of all college graduates in 1961. Since the purpose of our research is to uncover the correlates and determinants of apostasy, it makes little difference whether we deal with the weighted or the unweighted samples. For simplicity's sake, we shall deal primarily with the unweighted sample, especially when we are examining the correlates of apostasy. However, the absolute amount of apostasy in each religion is also an important consideration, particularly for purposes of comparing the rates in the various religions. Since Jews were more likely to attend large colleges, they are slightly oversampled, and thus, to permit proper comparisons among the religions, it is essential that we deal with the weighted sample. In short, on three occasions in the subsequent analysis, we will deal with the *weighted* samples, when we consider the apostasy rates for each religion in 1961, in 1964 (Chapter 7), and in 1968 (Chapter 8). On all other occasions, the analysis will be based on the *unweighted* samples.

According to the unweighted sample, 58 percent of the college graduates in 1961 were raised as Protestants, 25 percent as Catholics, 11 percent as Jews, 3 percent in other religions, and 3 percent in no religion. By the time they were ready to graduate from college, 50 percent still identified themselves as Protestants (a fall of 8 percentage points), 24 percent as Catholics, 9 percent as Jews, 4 percent as some other religion, and those identifying with no religion increased to 13 percent. These figures report only the net change between religion of origin and current religion. To some extent, the losses in any religious group have been compensated by conversions to that religion. The loss rate for each religion emerges when religion of origin is related to current religion, as is done in Table 1.1.

Table 1.1: Religion of Origin by Current Religion Based on the Weighted Sample (in percentages)

	Religion of Origin		
Religion as Seniors	**Jews**	**Protestants**	**Catholics**
Same	85	85	91
Convert	2	4	3
Apostate	13	11	6
	100	100	100
N**	(3,622)	(18,937)	(8,175)

*Students raised in other religions and no religion are omitted from this and all subsequent tables.

**The conventional format of tabulations is to show in parentheses the base figures on which the percentages are computed. This is not the case here. The percentages were calculated on the basis of the weighted Ns, whereas the Ns reported here are the actual number in each religion who participated in the study. The weighted Ns are much larger, but since we will deal with unweighted Ns in analyzing correlates of apostasy, we will always report the unweighted Ns even when we present percentages based on the weighted sample.

Table 1.1 is based on the weighted sample intended to represent all college seniors in 1961. It shows the retention and loss rates for each religion, the latter consisting of those who convert or apostatize. The Jews and Protestants show the same retention rates of 85 percent, but the Jews are slightly more likely to be apostates, leading all the religions in this respect with a rate of 13 percent, whereas the Protestants have a higher conversion rate, 4 percent. The Catholics have the highest retention rate, 91 percent, and the smallest apostasy rate, 6 percent. In the subsequent analysis, the relatively few converts in each religion will not be studied.

ON THE MEANING OF APOSTASY

We have already suggested that apostasy means both rejection of religious beliefs and affiliation with a religious category based on an ascribed status. This concept of apostasy is particularly appropriate for the Jews who more than the Protestants and Catholics view their religious affiliation as an ethnic status. Fortunately, data can be brought to bear on these components of apostasy. At one point in the survey, students were asked to describe the extent of their religiosity, that is, whether they considered themselves very religious, fairly religious, neither religious nor nonreligious, fairly nonreligious or very nonreligious. By relating these responses to the retention of a religious identity and its obverse, apostasy, we learn something about the significance of religiosity for these group identifications. These data are presented in Table 1.2.

Table 1.2: Proportion of Identifiers and Apostates Who Are Very or Fairly Religious by Religion of Origin (in percentages)

Religion of Seniors	Religion of Origin: Jewish	Protestant	Catholic
Identifier	45 (3,042)	78 (15,797)	90 (7,310)
Apostate	4 (458)	10 (2,185)	10 (550)

Protestants and Catholics exhibit a strong association between religiosity and identification. Almost four out of every five Protestant identifiers describe themselves as religious, while the figure increases to nine out of every ten among Catholics. But the pattern is different among Jews.

Fewer than half of the Jewish identifiers consider themselves to be religious. In short, it appears that for Jewish college seniors, religion is not the basis for their identity as Jews. We may conclude from this finding that Jewish apostates not only reject religion, but reject their ties to the Jewish community as well. Among Christians, religiosity and identity are more closely associated. Yet, 22 percent of the Protestants who identify themselves as Protestants report that they are not religious; among Catholics, this group constitutes 10 percent of the identifiers. Table 1.2 makes clear that group belongingness, independent of religiosity, is important to Jewish identity. This same force plays some role in Protestant identity and is even to be found in Catholic identity, though to a much smaller extent. In other words, religiosity is particularly important to Catholic identity, somewhat less so to Protestant identity, and least important to Jewish identity.

Before leaving Table 1.2, we should note that not all apostates lack a religious commitment. A minute fraction of the apostates among Jews, 4 percent, and a small fraction among both Protestant and Catholic apostates, 10 percent, describe themselves as religious. Had these students been sampled in the seventies rather than the early sixties, we might conclude that they were disciples of the new messianic, fundamentalistic religions that have attracted a number of the young. Perhaps these early-sixties religious apostates were the precursors of the current true believers in far-out sects.

Theoretical Orientations to Apostasy

Apostasy among college graduates, then, is relatively rare. Most students retain, in differing degrees in each of the three major religions, their original religious identification. Furthermore, we now know that this identification encompasses, as Herberg and Lenski had suggested, both a religious and communal component. How, then, might we explain the clearly deviant pattern of apostasy? Since religiosity is an important component of religious identification, it should follow that those who have lost religious faith would tend to abandon a religious identification. This is the secularization conception of apostasy which presupposes cognitive conflicts between secular and religious views of the world that are resolved in favor of the secular one. The research problem posed by this orientation is one of identifying the types of individuals who are likely to experience this conflict and resolve it in favor of the secular view of the world. Are they the graduating seniors committed to science as a vocation? Are they the most intellectually oriented students? Are they the ones most sensitive to a discrepancy between religious and scientific interpretations of the world?

Both the religiosity and communal components of religious identification suggest other interpretations of apostasy. The person who is ready to sever his ties with any major institutional sector of society—in this case, a religious community—is apt to be the alienated person—a type of continuing interest to sociologists.[9] Through the years, alienation has taken on many meanings, and in the past decade or so several sociologists have attempted to clarify the concept. The most notable effort is that of Melvin Seeman, who specified five distinct meanings of the term in the sociological literature.[10] According to Seeman, alienation has referred to "powerlessness," "meaninglessness," "isolation," "self-estrangement," and "normlessness." These types of alienation are not all relevant to apostasy among college seniors. For example, college seniors are not yet in the labor force, and the chances are that they are oriented to a professional career. Self-estrangement or work alienation, as Seeman elaborates this concept, is therefore not apt to be a significant form of alienation for them. Nor does "normlessness," the readiness to use illegitimate means to achieve legitimate goals, seem relevant to the population of college graduates who have had access to the socially approved means of education for achieving culturally approved ends. By the same token, we should not expect "powerlessness" to be a significant form of alienation among college seniors on the grounds that they have not yet had an opportunity to measure how powerless or powerful they are in spheres of life. The remaining two types of alienation identified by Seeman, "meaninglessness" and "isolation" seem most relevant to apostasy among college seniors. "Meaninglessness" relates to the kind of cognitive conflict between religious and secular views of the world we have touched upon and is thus relevant to the secularization hypothesis of apostasy. Of particular significance is the type of alienation that Seeman identifies as "isolation" and that Middleton, building on Seeman's work, translates as "cultural estrangement."[11] The person who experiences this type of alienation is estranged from the dominant values of society as expressed in popular culture, and presumably from many of the major institutions of society. The individuals who suffer from "meaninglessness" or from "isolation" or "cultural estrangement" are apt to be in a state of rebellion against their institutional ties and origins. The classic example is provided by the child who has turned on his parents and is determined to do whatever his parents disapprove of, who grows into the adult in a state of rebellion, but this process can also apply to the political radical who is determined to change the core institutions of his society. Much of the data in this monograph lends substance to the hypothesis that alienation-rebellion is another path to apostasy. But it is doubtful that alienation-rebellion and secularization, the undermining of religiosity, exhaust the forces that lead to relinquishing a religious identity. The alienation-rebellion hypothesis has certain pejorative overtones; it implies that only those who are out of step with society succumb to apostasy, whereas the secularization hypothesis deals with the undermining of religious belief which is perhaps a sufficient basis for identification with a religious community but not a necessary one. A third theory of the processes leading to apostasy calls attention to yet another force undermining the communal dimension of religious identification, commitment to certain dominant values of modern society. As Parsons has pointed out, the dominant institutions of modern society, especially the occupational structure, are based on the values of universalism and achievement, as opposed to particularism and ascription.[12] Statuses based on achievement rather than on birth or ascription are increasingly important in determining one's location in society and defining one's self. The popular cocktail-party game of identifying one's conversational partner almost always focuses on an occupational identification and seldom on a religious one. Religion, being largely an ascribed status handed down from generation to generation, is less likely a basis for self-identification than such achieved statuses as occupation, education, economic wealth, and political power. The submergence of ascribed statuses, such as nationality, ethnicity, religion, and even race, is the underlying premise of the "melting-pot" thesis of American society. And if the continued salience of these ascribed statuses casts doubts on the "melting-pot" idea, it is nonetheless true that the thrust of an achievement-oriented society is to underplay ascribed statuses and to emphasize achieved ones. This concept of apostasy suggests that the students most committed to achievement and universalism, such as those oriented to careers in the sciences or the academic community, should be particularly prone to apostasy.

In summary, we have sketched out three theories of the processes that might lead to apostasy. The first, captured by the term "secularization," directs attention to the undermining of the religiosity component of identification. The second, alienation-rebellion, identifies a force that attacks both the religiosity and the communal dimensions of religious identification. And the third, commitment to the modern values of universalism-achievement, deals with the undermining of the communal basis for religious identification which rests on ascription and particularism, the polar opposites of the modern values.

The three theories of the processes leading to apostasy are closely related to each other, and much of the data in hand seem to support each of them. For example, we might suppose that the more intellectually oriented students are the ones who have most acutely experienced the clash between fundamental religious doctrine and the ideas of modern science and thus have been most susceptible to the pull of secularization. And precisely because they are committed to intellectualism, they should experience the type of alienation that leads to disassociation from the conventional values of the society. Finally, the intellectually oriented students are most likely to internalize the modern values of universalism and achievement and give less priority to statuses like religion, which are based on ascription. As this discussion implies, we shall have considerable difficulty supporting one rather than another theory of apostasy. Nonetheless, we shall present the findings and note which of these theories any given finding seems to support.

NOTES

1. Gallup Opinion Index, Report No. 30, "Religion in America 1976."
2. Rose Goldsen, Maurice Rosenberg, Robin Williams, and Edward Suchman, *What College Students Think,* Princeton, N.J.: Van Nostrand, 1960.
3. Ibid, p. 181.
4. Clyde Parker, "The Religious Development of College Students," in Merton P. Strommen, ed., *Research on Religious Development: A Comprehensive Handbook,* New York: Hawthorne, 1971.
5. These studies were done mainly in the fifties and sixties. For the seventies, new studies are needed of the religious revival and the emergence of fundamental religious movements on the fringe of the college population. No one knows whether the "Jesus freaks" and the others are passing phenomena. In any case, their discovery of religion represents a sharp departure from the three established religions, which regard these youngsters as drop-outs.
6. The 33,782 who returned completed questionnaires in the spring of 1961 represented 82.2 percent of the intended sample. Over the three year period, NORC received at least one response to its yearly survey from 37,608, or 91.5 percent, of the intended sample of 41,000. This study, however, is concerned only with those who responded in 1961.
7. This was first done in an earlier NORC study of college students. See James A. Davis, *Stipends and Spouses,* Chicago: Aldine, 1961. See also, Joseph Zelan, "Religious Apostasy, Higher Education and Occupational Choice," *Sociology of Education,* Vol. 41, No. 4, Fall 1968.
8. The appendix deals with the converts and compares them with the identifiers and apostates.
9. Greeley, dealing with the same data that we do, attempts to explain apostasy in terms of alienation. See Andrew Greeley, *Religion and Career,* Chapter 8, Chicago: Aldine, 1963.

10. Melvin Seeman, "On the Meaning of Alienation," *American Sociological Review,* December 1959, pp. 783-791.

11. Russell Middleton, "Alienation, Race and Education," *American Sociological Review,* December 1963, pp. 973-977.

12. Talcott Parsons, *The Social System,* New York: Free Press, 1950.

Chapter 2

SOCIAL ORIGINS AND APOSTASY

This chapter examines the relevance of the students' social origins and other characteristics acquired before college, for the phenomenon of apostasy. We shall first look at the home town of these students from the viewpoint of its regional location and size to see if apostasy in this population is geographically linked. We shall also compare the apostasy rates of males and females. But the chief concern will be with the student's family. Religion, after all, is very much a family affair. In the great majority of cases, one's religious identity is determined by the religion of one's parents. To have been raised as a Jew, Protestant, or Catholic implies that either one or both of one's parents think of themselves as Jews, Protestants, or Catholics. Thus, the student raised in a particular religion who answers "none" to current religious status is willy nilly disassociating himself from his parents. Whether he does so out of rebellion, shame, indifference, or (for those from a minority religion) the desire to assimilate, his apostasy would seem, in part at least, to be a commentary on his relationship with his family. Information is available on both the socio-economic status of the student's family and the quality of his relations with his parents. The data to be presented perform more than a descriptive function. As we shall see, they permit testing some theories about the underlying causes of apostasy, in particular the significance of the "modernity" and "alienation" hypotheses.

Region and Home-Town Size: The Ecology of Apostasy

It is widely assumed that the appeal of religion varies in different sections of the country. The South is known as the "Bible belt" and fundamentalist religions thrive in that area. Presumably, those raised in the South should have religious identities more strongly impressed upon them than those raised in other sections of the country. The religious spirit might also be assumed to be quite strong in the farm-belt regions and in New England, which was initially settled by religious groups in colonial times. But whether the patterns of apostasy in each religion are the same across the country is not at all clear. In the Jewish community there has been much concern about the fate of Jews in regions sparsely settled by co-religionists. There is some evidence that the Jewish intermarriage rate is higher in small towns and places with relatively few Jews.[1] Such findings suggest that Jewish identity is more likely to flourish in those parts of the country with heavy concentrations of Jews, for only large Jewish communities can support the variety of Jewish institutions that help sustain a Jewish identity. According to this line of reasoning, the Jewish apostasy rate, and even the Catholic rate, should be high in the South and West North Central regions, since they have relatively few Jews and Catholics.

The facts of the matter are shown in Table 2.1.

The data do not support the thesis that the size of the religious community is relevant to the maintenance of a religious identity. The number of Jewish, Protestant, or Catholic students from a particular region (shown in parentheses)

Table 2.1: Apostasy by Region in which Student Was Raised (in percentages)

Region	Jewish	Protestant	Catholic
New England	9 (200)	20 (555)	5 (858)
Middle Atlantic	14 (1,934)	14 (2,773)	8 (2,385)
East North Central	13 (384)	13 (3,438)	5 (1,812)
West North Central	10 (94)	10 (1,666)	5 (388)
South	8 (102)	6 (3,782)	4 (379)
Mountain and West*	17 (208)	16 (3,070)	14 (585)

*Although we have grouped the Mountain States, Hawaii, and Alaska with the Far West, relatively few students from any religious group come from these states. The overwhelming majority in this category are from California, Oregon and Washington.

reflects roughly the size of the religious community in that region. The largest concentration of Jews in America is in the Middle Atlantic states and these states contribute fully two-thirds of all the Jewish college seniors in the sample. Yet the Jewish apostasy rate for this region is the second highest of all.

In contrast, the data do support the argument of regional differences in the emphasis placed upon religion. The South turns out to have the lowest apostasy rates and this is true not only for the Protestants who dominate the Southern scene, but for Jews and Catholics as well, who comprise distinct minorities in the South. The West, on the other hand, clearly emerges as the region with the least commitment to religion. Jews and Catholics raised in the West have the highest apostasy rates, the Catholic figure being fully twice as great as the overall Catholic apostasy rate of 7 percent, and the Protestants from the West show the second highest rate for their religion.

The one anomaly of Table 2.1 is the unusually high apostasy rate for the Protestants from New England. The Jewish and Catholic rates in New England are rather low and in keeping with the notion that the religious spirit is still fairly strong there. But, of course, the Protestants should be the backbone of the New England religious spirit, if there is one, and yet the Protestant students from this region have the highest apostasy rate.

Several other observations about Table 2.1 are in order. It may be noted that, with the exception of New England, the Jewish and Protestant rates are virtually identical in each region. That the overall Jewish apostasy rate is slightly higher than the Protestant rate might well be related to the fact that the great majority of Jews come from the Middle Atlantic region, which happens to be a region of fairly high apostasy. The Catholics show a consistently low apostasy rate in every region except the West. Their patterns are a further refutation of the argument based on the size of the religious community, for the second highest Catholic rate occurs in the Middle Atlantic states, the region that produces the largest number of Catholic students.

Next to the South, the region most conducive to the maintenance of religious identification appears to be the West North Central, which encompasses many of the major agricultural states. These regional patterns suggest that urbanization may well be one of the forces at work weakening religious identification. Most large cities in America are located in the two regions with the highest apostasy rates, the Middle Atlantic and the Far West.

The significance of home-town size for apostasy can be seen in Table 2.2. For cities of 100,000 or more, we have distinguished suburbs from central cities. This permits us to examine not only the role of urbanization, but that of the suburban trend as well.

Table 2.2: Apostasy by Size of Home Town (in percentages)

Size of Home Town	Jewish Rate	Protestant Rate	Catholic Rate
Farm, rural	6 (47)	9 (4,658)	6 (894)
City (under 50,000)	10 (120)	11 (3,910)	8 (995)
City (50,000-99,999)	11 (247)	13 (2,233)	5 (1,106)
City (100,000-499,999)	9 (185)	12 (1,267)	7 (656)
Suburb of city (100,000-499,999)	12 (148)	13 (1,289)	6 (568)
City (500,000-2 million)	12 (282)	14 (970)	7 (676)
Suburb of city (500,000-2 million)	14 (273)	16 (1,581)	6 (865)
City (over 2 million)	14 (1,666)	17 (666)	8 (1,214)
Suburb of city (over 2 million)	16 (553)	19 (1,499)	9 (931)

The expected relationship between urbanization and apostasy is found for both Jews and Protestants, but not at all for Catholics. With one slight deviation for cities between 100,000 and 500,000, the Jewish and Protestant apostasy rates steadily increase with size of home town. Suburbanization is also related to Jewish and Protestant apostasy. For cities of 100,000 or more, the suburban areas have higher Jewish and Protestant apostasy rates than the corresponding central city. The often heard speculation about the revival of religion in the suburbs would seem (at least for this population of college seniors) to be largely a myth. On the contrary, the metropolis and the suburbs surrounding it are much less fertile soil for religious identification than the small towns and rural areas. This, of course, is in keeping with the trend toward secularization in Western society. The dominant values of modern society, universalism and achievement, find their strongest expression in the metropolis and suburbs.[2]

Perhaps the striking finding in Table 2.2 is not that urbanization is related to apostasy among Jews and Protestants, but rather that Catholics are virtually immune to this trend. As can be seen from the third column, the Catholic apostasy rate hardly varies at all with size of community nor does growing up in a suburb, rather than a central city, have an effect on Catholic identification. This may mean that the Catholic community has been more successful in adapting to urbanization and its related phenomena, somehow integrating both ascribed and achieved identification, or perhaps that the Catholic community has been better able to insulate itself from the value system of an urban society in which achieved statuses are stressed.[3]

Before leaving Table 2.2, it may be noted from the base figures that Protestantism is very much a small-town and rural phenomenon in America. More than half of these Protestant graduates grew up in rural areas or in towns under 50,000, and it is these rural and small-town Protestants that have the lowest apostasy rate. In contrast, more than two-thirds of the Jews come from metropolitan areas with populations of more than 2 million, the very areas with relatively high apostasy rates. Were the distribution of Jews and Protestants similar with respect to home-town size, the Protestants would clearly have a much higher overall apostasy rate. In other words, the overall Protestant apostasy rate is virtually as large as the Jewish rate in spite of the fact that proportionately more Protestants were raised in communities in which religion is still a strong force.

Sex Differences in Apostasy

Previous studies have established that women tend to be more religious than men. Thus, it has been shown that women are more likely to attend church and to believe in God.[4] Apart from religiosity, we might expect that women are more inclined to retain a religious identity on communal grounds. The women's liberation movement notwithstanding, the woman's role is still defined in more traditional terms in modern society than that of the man. Even the college-educated woman is not under as much pressure as her male counterpart to be achievement oriented. She can still fulfill society's expectations by being a good wife and mother. On this basis, it would seem that an ascribed identity, such as religious affiliation, is more compatible with the role of the woman than that of the man. Furthermore, to the extent that apostasy represents, in part, a break with the family, we might expect daughters, who traditionally are closer to parents than are sons, to be less likely to make this break.

The expected sex differential shows up in each religion, but it is more pronounced among Protestants and Catholics than it is among Jews. For the former groups, the male apostasy rate is almost twice as large as the female rate (15 percent of the Protestant men compared with 8 percent of the Protestant women, and 9 percent of the Catholic men compared with 5 percent of the Catholic women apostatize). Jewish women, in contrast, are only somewhat less likely to apostatize than the Jewish men (11 percent compared with 14 percent).

Socio-Economic Status and Apostasy

There has been considerable speculation, especially with respect to Jews, as to the effect of social class on adherence to a religion. There are at least two perspectives from which theories about such a connection can be generated. The first, which applies mainly to Jews, is based on the minority status of the religion and emphasizes the pressures on the members toward assimilation into the majority culture as both a condition and consequence of success. The variant of this theory, which sees assimilation as a *condition* for success, is captured in the stereotype of the "allrightnik" in Jewish folklore. This is the person who views his Jewishness as a handicap in the struggle for success and thus rejects it in order to ease the long journey of social climbing towards the goal he has set for himself. According to this version of assimilationist theory it should be the Jewish college graduate of working-class origins who is most ready to be an apostate. Whatever the validity of this line of reasoning, it would be extremely difficult to prove with the data on hand. If such "allrightniks" are really represented in the sample, it is quite likely that they would not only say they currently have no religion but would even deny that they were raised as Jews, and would thus be lost to our measure of Jewish apostasy altogether.[5]

The second variant of assimilationist theory would lead to the expectation that it is the more well-to-do in the minority group, those who have already made it, who experience pressure to relinquish their religious identity. The stereotype of the "nouveau riche" is appropriate here to capture the person who loses his religious identity after he has achieved some economic success. For one thing, such a person is more likely to be accepted by the dominant group than his co-religionists who have not made it, and thus finds it easier to assimilate should he choose to. Secondly, in order to match his economic success with social success, he may be more ready to loosen his identity with a minority religious group.

The assimilationist theory in its two variations seems most applicable to Jews and, to some extent, to Catholics, since they too belong to a minority religion in America. Such a theory, however, can have no relevance for Protestant apostasy precisely because Protestants are the majority group.

But there is a second perspective from which a connection between religious identification and social class can be viewed. As we have already noted, religion is largely an ascribed social status. To the extent that achieved statuses take precedence over ascribed statuses, we may expect that religious identities are weaker in precisely those groups which have most internalized achievement values. Since we are dealing with a population of college seniors, which almost by definition has strong achievement values, it might seem that we have located a constant rather than a variable. But it is quite possible that those young men and women who grew up in successful families were more exposed to achievement values and had as models parents who themselves placed greater stress on achieved than on ascribed statuses. According to this view, the products of more successful families, whatever the religion, should be more likely to apostatize, reflecting in themselves the weaker religious identities of their parents.

We may note in passing a third theory that would also predict a positive relationship between apostasy and social class, the Marxian notion of "religion as the opiate of the masses." To the extent that one function of religion is to make life meaningful and manageable for those who are most deprived, then, of course, religious fervor should be strongest in working- and lower-class families and weakest in upper-class families.

Data are available for characterizing the class position of the students' families in terms of the three traditional indicators: father's occupation, education and income. Rather than combining these into an index of socio-economic status, we shall examine each separately to see what, if any, bearing it has on apostasy. Table 2.3 shows how father's occupation is related to apostasy in each religion.

The deductions derived from assimilationist theory are not at all borne out by the data. Jewish and Catholic students from

Table 2.3: Apostasy Rates by Father's Occupation (in percentages)

Father's Occupation	Jewish Rate	Protestant Rate	Catholic Rate
Professional	15 (807)	15 (4,901)	7 (1,698)
Proprietor, manager	13 (1,453)	13 (4,365)	7 (1,934)
Sales, clerical	13 (570)	12 (2,109)	6 (1,049)
Blue collar	12 (643)	11 (4,779)	8 (2,853)
Farm, farm worker	0 (5)	5 (1,705)	5 (245)

lower social origins are not more likely to apostatize than those from higher social origins. The "achievement theory" fares somewhat better. According to this view, apostasy should be greater in all religions for those from higher social positions. This theory would predict that the relationship holds for Protestants as well as those from minority religions. And, indeed, the expectation finds some support from the Protestant pattern; the Jewish pattern is similar, although much weaker; but as was the case with urbanization, we find no pattern at all among the Catholics. The capacity of the Catholic community to retain the loyalty of its college-educated youth appears to be just as strong for those reared in the professional class as in the working class. The strength of religion in rural settings is confirmed in this table where we see that the Christian sons and daughters of farmers have the lowest apostasy rates. (Only five Jewish students were children of farmers and none of them apostatized.)

The other two indicators of socio-economic status show similar results. No matter what the father's income or education, Catholic apostasy remains constant, varying from 6 to 8 percentage points. Wealthier and better-educated fathers are associated with higher apostasy among the Protestants, whereas, among the Jews, the patterns are more irregular. On balance, it is primarily the Protestants who show some relationship between socio-economic status and apostasy.

The Quality of Parental Relations and Apostasy

As we noted at the outset of the chapter, apostasy, to some extent at least, is likely to represent a break with the family of origin. To have been raised by one's parents in a particular religion and now to feel no identification with a religious community might well be symptomatic of familial strain and disassociation from parents. From this perspective, apostasy is to be viewed as a form of rebellion against parents. Whether there is any merit to this notion can be investigated with the data on hand.

One indication of the closeness of the relationship between these college seniors and their parents is the degree to which they take into account the advice of their parents when making career decisions. Presumably, in close-knit families, the child is ready to consult his parents on such an important decision, and parents, especially—as the stereotype would have it—Jewish parents, are ready to offer such advice. Thus, if students report that the opinions of their parents had little or no importance in their career decisions, we might assume some alienation from parents. Table 2.4 presents the relationship between valuing parental advice and apostasy for the three religious groups.

Table 2.4: Apostasy Rates by Importance of Parental Advice on Career Decisions (in percentages)

Parental Advice	Jewish Rate	Protestant Rate	Catholic Rate
Very important	5 (706)	6 (3,281)	2 (1,523)
Fairly important	11 (1,525)	9 (7,362)	4 (3,210)
Unimportant	21 (995)	19 (4,863)	12 (2,017)
Never had	22 (245)	16 (2,106)	13 (983)

In each religion, apostasy increases sharply as parental advice is less valued. The pattern is virtually as strong for Catholics as it is for Jews and Protestants (although apostasy is less frequent among Catholics on all levels of importance). Among Protestants, never receiving parental advice is not quite as conducive to apostasy as considering such advice unimportant. But this result does not really detract from the pattern, for not to receive any advice from parents is more likely to reflect the style of life of the family than strain in the parental relation. Many parents, particularly Protestant parents, undoubtedly believe as a matter of principle that their children should make their own career decisions and thus refrain from offering advice. More significant is the value placed on such advice when it is offered. Those who value it highly undoubtedly feel closer to their parents and, as the data show, closeness to parents measured in this way is strongly related to identification in all religious groups.

In the questionnaire administered in the fourth wave of the survey, three years after these college seniors had graduated, a series of questions was asked which dealt much more directly with the quality of parental relations during the time that the respondents were growing up in the family setting. On the assumption that their judgments would have been much the same had they been asked these questions three years earlier, we shall relate these data to apostasy at the time of graduation. Unfortunately, almost a third of the original sample failed to respond on the fourth wave and so we shall be dealing with substantially fewer cases. But the initial sample was so large that this loss is not likely to affect the results in any material way.

The respondents were asked to evaluate their childhood relations with their parents on several dimensions. On each, they had to report whether they enjoyed good relations with both parents, with one but not the other, or with neither parent. The items asked about the parent that the respondent most admired, the parent who best understood him, the parent he enjoyed being with more and the parent he tried hardest to please. We assume that the answer "both parents" signifies the closest familial relationship and the response "neither parent," the greatest degree of alienation, with the choice of "only one parent" standing in between. If closeness of the parental relationship is important for maintaining an identity with the religious community, we should find that these items are related to apostasy and indeed they are. In every instance, the response "neither parent" is associated with much more apostasy than the response "both equally." This is true in every religious group. For example, fully 20 percent of the Catholics who claimed they did not admire either parent apostatized, compared with only 5 percent of those who admired both equally.

The comparable figures for Protestants are 29 and 9 percent and for Jews, 29 and 8 percent. Similar patterns hold for the other three items.

Since each of these indicators of closeness to family is strongly related to the others, we have combined them into an index of the quality of familial relations. (The five possible scale scores have been reduced to three for purposes of this analysis.) Table 2.5 shows how this index is related to apostasy.

Table 2.5: Apostasy by Quality of Parental Relations (in percentages)

Quality of Parental Relations	Jews	Protestants	Catholics
Good (score 4)	8 (1,069)	8 (6,997)	4 (2,670)
Fair (score 2,3)	14 (677)	14 (3,235)	7 (1,278)
Poor (score 0,1)	28 (342)	26 (1,055)	18 (516)

As this table shows, apostasy increases sharply in each religious group as relations with parents deteriorate.

The data presented in this chapter on the social origins of the college graduates have lent support to two of the broad theories of apostasy outlined in the previous chapter: commitment to the values of achievement and universalism, with the consequent undermining of commitments based on ascription and particularism, and the alienation-rebellion thesis which views apostates as rejecting the dominant values and institutional spheres of society. In keeping with the first view were the findings showing that among Jews and Protestants apostasy was related to urbanization and suburbanization and was more prevalent in the more industrialized regions of the country, areas in which the values of universalism and achievement are more deeply embedded. But these findings did not hold for Catholics.

The sex difference in apostasy, the fact that women were more likely to retain their religious identity than men, is also in keeping with the "universalism-achievement" theory, since women are under less pressure than men to live up to achievement norms. The data showing that social class is positively related to apostasy among Protestants, and to some extent among Jews, provides further support for the achievement hypothesis since achievement norms are more likely to be internalized in the successful strata, but, again, this pattern did not hold for the Catholics, suggesting that Catholic apostasy may have different wellsprings from Jewish and Protestant apostasy.

The alienation-rebellion theory found confirmation in the findings showing that apostasy was linked to poor parental relations, a situation likely to result in rebellion against the family of origin. The findings bearing on this hypothesis held true for all three religious groups, the Catholics as well as the Protestants and Jews. In subsequent chapters, we shall uncover a number of other correlates of apostasy, but, by and large, these will fall into one or another of the three major theories outlined in the previous chapter.

NOTES

1. Erich Rosenthal, "Jewish Intermarriage in Indiana," *American Jewish Yearbook,* Vol. 68, 1967, pp. 243-264.

2. The early theorists of city life made a big point of the breakdown of primary-group ties and the anonymity and isolation of city dwellers. See, for example, Louis Wirth, "Urbanism as a Way of Life," *American Journal of Sociology,* Vol. 44, July 1938. This view of the city would suggest that urbanites suffer from many of the symptoms of anomie and alienation. But even if there is some merit to this view of the urban community, it would hardly apply to suburbia, which is seen as having many of the virtues of small-town life. Our interpretation of Table 2.2 thus rests more on the culture of modernity than on alienation per se.

3. In later chapters, we shall examine whether this apparent capacity of the Catholic community to resist the secularizing pressures of urbanization can be understood in part by the kinds of colleges Catholic youth attend and the kinds of career choices they make.

4. See Charles W. Mueller and Weldon T. Johnson, "Socio-Economic Status and Religious Participation," *American Sociological Review,* Vol. 40, No. 6, December 1975, pp. 785-800.

5. Such types are more likely to be found among those who indicated that they were raised in some other religion, or in no religion at all.

Chapter 3

SELF-IMAGES, VALUE ORIENTATIONS, AND APOSTASY

Apostasy, as we have seen, is relatively rare in each religion, even among these college seniors. Precisely because it is so rare, we might expect that apostates have rather different personalities from those who maintain their religious identity. This chapter examines a number of personality attributes, as defined by the students themselves, that identify the ways in which the self-images, attitudes and value-orientations of apostates differ from those of identifiers. Three broad attributes that touch upon the theories of apostasy presented in Chapter 1 will be analyzed for their connection with apostasy: the degree to which seniors consider themselves to be well-adjusted personalities, the degree to which they orient themselves to non-materialistic values, including intellectualism, and the degree to which they accept a radical political perspective toward society. The measures of these attributes will develop as we look at some of the information elicited in the questionnaires.

Self-Descriptions of Apostates and Identifiers

At one point, the students were presented with a list of thirty-three adjectives which might apply to them. They were asked to check "only those which are most characteristic of you as a person." The typical student chose eight to nine adjectives from the list. An analysis of these choices provides a picture of how apostates and identifiers view themselves and, at the same time, contributes to our understanding of the forces making for apostasy. It should be noted that when responses of apostates and identifiers are compared, differences of at least seven percentage points in at least two religious groups were found on only twelve of the thirty-three adjectives.[1] Such descriptions as

Table 3.1: Self-Descriptions More Characteristic of Identifiers than of Apostates (in percentages)

Characteristic	Identifiers	Apostates	Difference
Happy:			
Jews	39	26	13
Protestants	53	33	20
Catholics	46	28	18
Cooperative:			
Jews	58	41	17
Protestants	64	44	20
Catholics	60	42	18
Ambitious:			
Jews	59	47	12
Protestants	59	51	8
Catholics	56	51	5
Fun-Loving:			
Jews	43	34	9
Protestants	45	38	7
Catholics	45	38	7
Obliging:			
Jews	28	19	9
Protestants	29	24	5
Catholics	31	24	7

Base figures:	*Identifiers*	*Apostates*
Jews	3,083	465
Protestants	15,958	2,218
Catholics	7,387	566

"good-looking," "witty," "reserved," "easy-going," and "methodical" were chosen with about the same frequency by identifiers and apostates in each religion. It is instructive to examine the characteristics that do differentiate the apostates from the identifiers. Table 3.1 presents the five self-descriptions that were more frequently chosen by the identifiers.

The first thing to be noted about Table 3.1 is that the pattern is the same in all three religious groups. In every instance, the trait that differentiates apostates from identifiers in one religious group does so in the others. This is further evidence of the generality of apostasy and the forces producing it.

As for the items that were more popular with identifiers, the one that most sharply differentiates them from apostates is "happy." Whether unhappiness is a cause of apostasy or a consequence of it cannot, of course, be determined, but the often-heard claim that religion contributes to peace of mind finds some support here. Inspection of the adjectives listed in Table 3.1 suggests that the identifiers are more likely to consider themselves well-adjusted than are the apostates. To be happy, cooperative, fun-loving and obliging is to possess the conventional virtues of our middle-class society. "Ambitious" turns out to be a highly popular self-description in both groups, although it is even more characteristic of the identifiers. This, too, is in keeping with the "well-adjusted" syndrome, for in America ambition is a highly desirable trait.

Having seen the self-descriptions more popular with identifiers, let us now consider those chosen more frequently by the apostates. These appear in Table 3.2.

As in Table 3.1, we again see that the self-description chosen more frequently by apostates in one religion are also more characteristic of the apostates in the other religions. Just as "happy" differentiated identifiers from apostates most sharply in Table 3.1, the self-description "intellectual" performs this function in Table 3.2. In every religion, the label "intellectual" is substantially more popular with the apostates.

These various self-descriptions fall into two categories. The first three–intellectual, idealistic, and cultured–refer to values that are held in high esteem, especially in the Jewish

Table 3.2: Self-Descriptions More Characteristic of Apostates than of Identifiers (in percentages)

Characteristic	Identifiers	Apostates	Difference
Intellectual:			
Jews	25	46	-21
Protestants	16	34	-18
Catholics	18	35	-17
Idealistic:			
Jews	39	49	-10
Protestants	29	40	-11
Catholics	34	40	- 6
Cultured:			
Jews	27	37	-10
Protestants	18	24	- 6
Catholics	20	27	- 7
Rebellious:			
Jews	8	19	-11
Protestants	6	17	-11
Catholics	7	20	-13
Moody:			
Jews	28	44	-16
Protestants	19	31	-12
Catholics	22	33	-11
Lazy:			
Jews	13	19	- 6
Protestants	7	17	-10
Catholics	9	17	- 8
Impetuous:			
Jews	12	19	- 7
Protestants	7	14	- 7
Catholics	9	15	- 6

Base Figures:	*Identifiers*	*Apostates*
Jews	3,083	465
Protestants	15,958	2,218
Catholics	7,387	566

community (they are chosen more frequently by the Jews than by the Protestants and Catholics), even though they are not widely shared in our materialistic culture. They reflect the kind of lofty values that are admired in others, though they are not considered to be practical by most Americans. These values bear on two of the three theories of apostasy, secularization and alienation. Those committed to intellectualism, in particular, are likely to experience strain between religious and secular views of the world, and those who accept values that are *not* commonly held in society are apt to be manifesting the type of alienation that Seeman identifies as "isolation" and others have called "cultural estrangement," the rejection of the "goals or beliefs that are highly valued in a given society."[2]

The last four adjectives more characteristic of apostates than identifiers are of a different order. "Rebellious," "moody," "lazy," and "impetuous" all refer to negative traits symptomatic of maladjustment and neurosis. In his analysis of the concept of "alienation," Nettler, who defines alienation as being out of tune with one's society, predicts that the alienated are more likely to be neurotic.[3] The portrait of the apostate that emerges from these self-descriptions is that of an alienated person committed to intellectuality, idealism, and culture, values that are somewhat deviant in our materialistic society, and in keeping with the common stereotype of those committed to such values, the apostate is more likely to be an emotionally troubled person.

A Note on the Assimilationist Theory of Jewish Apostasy

It is widely believed in the Jewish community that any weakening in Jewish identify is motivated by the desire to assimilate with the dominant social groups of American society. According to this view, the Jewish apostate, in moving *from* the Jewish community, is moving *toward* the dominant Christian community which, in America, means Protestantism. But the data presented in Tables 3.1 and 3.2 belie this interpretation of apostasy. We have already noted that apostates in each religion are differentiated from the identifiers in the same way. In other words, they are moving in the same direction away from the culture of conventional society. Table 3.3 presents the data rearranged so as to make this point clearer.

The first column in Table 3.3 shows the percentage of Protestant identifiers choosing each characteristic to describe themselves. The other columns have been arranged to reflect

Table 3.3: Self-Descriptions of Identifiers and Apostates in Each Relation Arranged to Test the Assimilationist Hypothesis (in percentages)

	Identifiers			Apostates		
Characteristic	Protestants	Catholics	Jews	Protestants	Catholics	Jews
Happy	53	46	42	33	28	28
Cooperative	64	60	60	44	42	43
Ambitious	59	56	59	51	51	50
Fun-loving	45	45	45	38	38	36
Obliging	29	31	30	24	24	20
Intellectual	16	18	27	34	35	49
Idealistic	29	34	42	40	40	51
Cultured	18	20	28	24	27	39
Moody	19	22	39	31	33	47
Rebellious	6	7	9	17	20	21
Lazy	7	9	14	17	17	20
Impetuous	7	9	13	14	15	20

closeness to the Protestant identifiers. By reading across each row it can readily be seen that the Jewish apostates are at the opposite pole from the Protestant identifiers. When Jews apostatize, they are clearly not taking on characteristics of Protestant identifiers. In every instance the responses of the Jewish identifiers are much closer to those of the Protestant identifiers than are those of Jewish apostates. In fact, in most instances, the Jewish identifiers are closer to the Protestant identifiers than are the Protestant apostates. The same is true for the Catholics. Table 3.3 makes quite clear that the identifiers as a group, whatever their religion, tend to have similar traits and that the apostates, whatever their religion, have much in common. Rather than apostasy among Jews and Catholics representing a movement toward the mainstream of American society, apostasy in all religions would appear to be a movement from the mainstream.

Personality Traits as Determinants of Apostasy

So far, we have presented data on differences in the ways that identifiers and apostates view themselves. These self-descriptions overlap and can be used to develop indices of personality traits that might be viewed as determinants of apostasy. For example, the adjectives in Table 3.1 that suggest social adjustment–happy, cooperative, fun-loving, and obliging–are all positively related to each other. Similarly, the negative descriptions that suggest emotional disturbance–rebellious, moody, impetuous, and lazy–are positively related to each other, and the index of adjustment is, as we would expect, negatively related to the index of maladjustment. These various traits thus measure two extremes of the same underlying dimension: adjustment-maladjustment. Furthermore, the three attributes indicative of a commitment to nonmaterialistic values–intellectual, idealistic, and cultured–are also positively related to each other and can be used to measure orientation to "higher values."

When we earlier examined such variables as region, hometown size, socio-economic status of family, and quality of familial relations, it was rather clear that these attributes preceded apostasy in time and thus could be treated as determinants of apostasy. The causal sequence is less clear for such attributes as social adjustment or commitment to higher values. It is conceivable, for example, that poor adjustment developed after the apostate relinquished his identity with his religious community, and that his interest in the "higher values" also followed his apostasy. But on balance, it would seem that the causal connection is more likely to be in opposite direction. Emotional difficulties are not apt to spring up overnight, and an attraction to ideas, ideals, and culture is also likely to be the result of a long process of socialization. In any event, with full awareness of the ambiguities and uncertainties of the argument,

Table 3.4: Apostasy in Each Religion by Adjustment-Maladjustment Index (in percentages)

	Jews	Protestants	Catholics
Adjusted	7 (1,461)	8 (10,123)	4 (4,062)
Mixed	13 (1,386)	15 (5,984)	8 (2,833)
Maladjusted	25 (701)	26 (2,069)	15 (1,058)

we shall treat these personality traits as if they were determinants of apostasy rather than consequences of it. Table 3.4 shows how the index of social adjustment is related to apostasy in each religion.

For each religious group, social adjustment turns out to be strongly related to apostasy; the less adjusted the student, the more likely he is to apostatize. The results for Jews and Protestants are virtually identical; the same pattern is found for the Catholics, although they are less likely to apostatize whatever their level of adjustment. The maladjusted Catholics, in particular, have much less difficulty retaining their religious identification than the maladjusted Jews and Protestants. Since this trait might be considered a derivative of alienation, the alienation hypothesis finds support from Table 3.4.

Table 3.5 shows the relationship between "higher values" and apostasy.

Table 3.5: Apostasy in Each Religion by Commitment to Higher Values (in percentages)

Higher Value Commitment	Jews	Protestants	Catholics
Low	8 (968)	9 (9,715)	5 (3,990)
Medium	14 (1,197)	14 (5,527)	8 (2,498)
High	20 (1,383)	21 (2,934)	11 (1,465)

As expected, higher values are positively related to apostasy (although not as strongly as maladjustment) in all religious groups. And, again, we find that the relationship is somewhat stronger among the Jews and Protestants than among the Catholics, further evidence of the greater resistance of Catholics to apostasy-provoking forces.

That adjustment-maladjustment is related to apostasy is in keeping with the earlier finding of the link between the quality of parental relations and apostasy. Presumably, poor relations with parents contribute to emotional disturbance, and both findings might be subsumed under the disassociation-with-parents theory of apostasy, which in turn fits into the more general "alienation"-rebellion theory. But what are we to make of the association between "higher values" and apostasy? As suggested, sharing such values can be treated as a measure of the variant of alienation identified as social isolation or cultural estrangement. But it can also be argued that commitment to higher values is compatible with the dominant value-orientations of modernity—universalism and achievement—which prescribe that individuals are to be judged by what they have accomplished rather than the accidents of birth. In short, the apostates in each religion, in moving from the mainstream of current society, might be viewed as the harbingers of the future society in which universalism-achievement norms more completely supplant particularism-ascription norms.

Before leaving Tables 3.4 and 3.5, one further observation is in order. Close inspection of the base figures on which the percentages are computed will show that in each instance substantially more Jews than Protestants or Catholics have the trait associated with apostasy. Thus, some 17 percent of the Jews, in contrast with 12 percent of the Catholics and 10 percent of the Protestants, are in the maladjusted category. On "higher values" the religious differences are even more pronounced. Fully 39 percent of the Jews score high, compared with 18 percent of the Catholics and 16 percent of the Protestants. This predisposition of Jews toward the traits associated with apostasy is in keeping with what we found in the previous chapter. There we saw that Jews were more likely to come from large cities and those regions of the country with high apostasy rates. Since they have so many of the attributes associated with apostasy, Jews could be expected to have a much higher overall apostasy rate than Protestants or Catholics. But we already know that this is not so. The Jews tend to retain their identity in spite of their affinity for characteristics related to apostasy. The Protestant apostasy rate is as low as it is mainly because most Protestant students do not have the traits conducive to apostasy. Catholics, on the other hand, present a somewhat different picture. They are like the Protestants in having fewer of the characteristics conducive to apostasy. But even when they do possess these attributes, they are not as prone to apostasy as Jews and Protestants. Presumably, mechanisms are at work in the Catholic community which deflect the force of the apostasy-provoking traits.

Radical Perspectives and Apostasy

Almost all the revolutionary movements of the twentieth century have been antagonistic towards religion and religious institutions.[4] From the radical perspective, religion is part of the status quo that must be changed. Committed to nonmaterialistic values, prone to the traits of social maladjustment, the apostates might be presumed to be more radical in political outlook than the identifiers. Two items from the 1961 study permit an approximate measure of political radicalism, or, perhaps more accurately, of a critical stance toward the status quo. Needless to say, this trait, too, falls within the domain of the concept of alienation-rebellion.

The 1961 graduates were asked to rate themselves on a scale of conventionality, from very conventional to very unconventional. They were also asked to rate their political orientations from very liberal to very conservative. It is not surprising that apostasy in each religion is associated with unconventionality and political liberalism. Among Jews, apostasy increases from 4 percent to 33 percent as the students describe themselves as more and more unconventional; among Protestants the shift is from 3 percent to 40 percent and among Catholics from 2 percent to 33 percent. Similar patterns, although not as pronounced, are found for political orientation. In each religion, the very liberal are more likely to apostatize than the conservatives, with the exception of the very small number of very conservative Jews who have as high an apostasy rate as the liberal Jews. Among Protestants, apostasy increases from 10 percent among the conservatives to 26 percent among the very liberal, and among Catholics the conservative rate is 5 percent and the very liberal rate 13 percent. Again, Jews are more likely than Christians to have these apostasy-related traits. Thus, 40 percent of the Jews consider themselves to be fairly or very unconventional, compared with 30 percent of the Catholics and 29 percent of the Protestants. Fully 69 percent of the Jews say they are fairly or very liberal in contrast to 52 percent of the Catholics and 42 percent of the Protestants.

The very liberal in each religion are much more likely than those of other political orientations to define themselves as fairly or very unconventional. Thus, by combining these responses, we arrive at a measure of radicalism.[5]

Table 3.6 shows how this measure of political radicalism is related to apostasy in each religion.

Table 3.6: Apostasy in Each Religion by Radicalism (in percentages)

Radicalism	Jewish Rate	Protestant Rate	Catholic Rate
Low	6 (1,758)	6 (11,916)	4 (4,904)
Medium	17 (1,215)	22 (5,112)	11 (2,409)
High	30 (485)	45 (650)	23 (402)

This table summarizes what we have already learned about the association of the individual items with apostasy. The more radical the student's political orientation, the more likely he is to apostatize. This relationship is found in each religion and is particularly strong among the Protestants, where radicalism is an extremely deviant position.

So far, we have identified three attributes of students that are related to apostasy. One that we have called adjustment-maladjustment refers more to a basic personality trait; the others—commitment to nonmaterialistic higher values and political radicalism—can be thought of as value-orientations giving direction to the students' lives. All three can be thought of as indicators of "alienation" and to some extent "higher values" might be viewed as an indicator of achievement orientation. The question now arises as to whether these attributes are related to each other and, if so, whether they serve as independent determinants of apostasy.

It turns out that these personality attributes are related, but the relationships are fairly weak. Those committed to higher values are more likely to describe themselves in terms of the negative characteristics indicative of maladjustment, and they are more likely to have a radical political perspective. And the maladjusted are more likely than the adjusted to be radical. But the differences range only from 5 to 15 percentage points.

Since the apostasy-producing traits are related, we must consider their effect on apostasy independent of each other. Such analysis will also permit us to assess the relative importance of these attributes for apostasy. Table 3.7 shows the simultaneous effect of adjustment-maladjustment and higher values on apostasy for each religious group. This table is rather complex and should be studied carefully. It is divided into three parts, each part showing how these variables relate to apostasy within a particular religious group. Each entry in the table tells us the percentage of students with a particular combination of these traits who are apostates. The number of students who have the trait combination appears next to the percentage in parentheses. For example, the upper-left-hand cell in each part of the table identifies students who are well-adjusted and low on higher values. Among Jews, there are 659 such students and 4 percent of them are apostates. To simplify the reading of the table, we have computed for each column and each row the percentage difference between the extreme categories. These serve as a crude measure of the strength of the association between one of the attributes and apostasy when the other attribute is held constant.

Table 3.7: The Joint Effects of Adjustment-Maladjustment and Higher Values on Apostasy for Each Religious Group (in percentages)

Higher Values	Adjusted-Disturbed			
	Adjusted	Mixed	Disturbed	Difference
Jews				
Low	4 (659)	9 (480)	15 (244)	11
Medium	8 (478)	13 (485)	23 (234)	20
High	13 (324)	18 (421)	34 (223)	21
Difference	9	9	19	
Protestants				
Low	6 (6,003)	11 (2,854)	21 (858)	15
Medium	10 (2,889)	16 (1,907)	26 (731)	15
High	13 (1,231)	22 (1,223)	38 (480)	25
Difference	7	11	17	
Catholics				
Low	3 (2,256)	7 (1,323)	10 (411)	7
Medium	5 (1,226)	9 (910)	15 (362)	10
High	8 (580)	10 (600)	22 (285)	14
Difference	5	3	12	

As we read from the upper left to the lower right within each part of the table, we see that apostasy steadily increases in each religious group as the students possess more of these attributes. By reading across each row and down each column, it can be seen that each trait is related to apostasy when the other is held constant. These results indicate that adjustment-maladjustment and higher values have an *additive* effect upon apostasy in that each makes an independent contribution to the apostasy rate.

The percentage differences for each column and row tell us something about the strength of the relationship of one trait to apostasy when the other is held constant. By comparing percentage differences in the columns and rows in each sector of the table, it can be seen that adjustment-maladjustment is more strongly related to apostasy than is commitment to higher values. Thus, among Jews, the *average* difference in apostasy between those low and high on higher values is 14 percentage points, whereas the average difference between the adjusted and maladjusted is 17 percentage points. Among the Protestants, higher values yield an average difference of 12 percentage points, whereas for adjustment-maladjustment, the average difference is 18 percentage points. Among the Catholics the comparable figures are 7 and 10 percentage points.

There is still a further story told by the percentage differences in the columns and rows of Table 3.7. It will be noted that the effect of one of the traits on apostasy increases as the strength of the other trait increases. For example, among the well-adjusted Jews, higher values makes an impact of 9 percentage points on apostasy. (See the top lefthand column of the table.) Among the maladjusted Jews, the impact of higher values is 19 percentage points. Similarly, among the Jews who are low on higher values (see the top row), adjustment-maladjustment yields a percentage difference of 11 points, but among the Jews who are strongly committed to higher values this impact increases to 21 percentage points. The same patterns appear among the Protestants and Catholics. In short, when one of the traits is present to a strong degree, the other has a greater impact on apostasy than when the first trait is absent. This pattern indicates that adjustment-maladjustment and higher values not only have an additive effect upon apostasy, but that they also *interact* so as to reinforce each other's effect. Another way of saying this is that one trait serves as a *condition* for the effect of the other.

Results very similar to those in Table 3.7 emerge when the impact of radicalism on apostasy is considered first in the context of adjustment-maladjustment and then jointly with higher values. In each instance, the two determinants have a cumulative impact on apostasy in each religion and the impact of one trait is stronger when the other trait is present. Most importantly, these analyses show that radicalism has a more pronounced impact on apostasy than does either adjustment-maladjustment or higher values. Thus, among Jews, the average percentage difference in apostasy rates for radicalism when adjustment-maladjustment is held constant is 22 points; the comparable impact of adjustment-maladjustment is 12 points. For Protestants, these figures are 38 and 15 and for Catholics, 16 and 12. Radicalism far outdistances higher values as a determinant of apostasy. For Jews, it makes an average difference of 22 percentage points, in contrast with an 8 point difference for higher values. For Protestants, it makes an average difference of 36 points, compared with 10 points for higher values, and for Catholics these differences are 17 and 8 points respectively. By examining the impact of each trait in the context of the others, we have found that radicalism is the most powerful determinant of apostasy, followed by adjustment-maladjustment, with higher values in third place.

The cumulative impact of the three apostasy "germs" that we have been examining can be shown by combining these traits into a superindex which might be viewed as a measure of alienation in its several dimensions. The relationship of this "alienation" index to apostasy in each religion is shown in Table 3.8.

The more personality traits conducive to apostasy that the student possesses, the more likely he is to apostatize. This is particularly true among the Protestants. Their apostasy rate soars from only 9 percent among the majority who possess none of these traits to fully 67 percent among the tiny fraction who

Table 3.8: Apostasy According to Personality Predisposition on Index Presented Separately for Each Religion (in percentages)

Predisposition Index		Jewish Rate	Protestant Rate	Catholic Rate
Very low	(Score 0)	7 (1,866)	9 (12,973)	5 (5,359)
Medium low	(Score 1)	16 (1,141)	19 (3,937)	10 (1,913)
Medium high	(Score 2)	30 (372)	40 (696)	19 (388)
Very high	(Score 3)	39 (79)	67 (72)	49 (55)

possess all three. Catholics and Jews show the same pattern to lesser degrees. The base figures make quite clear that the majority in each religious group have none of these traits which no doubt explains why so many have no difficulty retaining their religious identity. Perhaps those truly dedicated to their religious identity are those who manage to cling to it in spite of their very high predisposition to relinquish it. Among Jews, this group constitutes a majority of those with all three predisposing traits (61 percent); among Catholics, slightly more than half were able to resist the "infection" of all three apostasy traits; among Protestants, only a minority of the most "infected" (33 percent) failed to succumb to apostasy.

Familial Relations, Personality Traits and Apostasy

In the previous chapter we saw that apostasy is closely related to the quality of parental relations. It should come as no surprise that the various attributes that we have been examining in this chapter are also related to the quality of parental relations for, to some extent, all of these attributes are related to the notion of alienation-rebellion. Thus, those who described their parental relations as poor rather than good are more likely to be maladjusted, committed to higher values and have a radical political orientation. Given these relationships, the question arises as to the independence and relative strength of the family experience and these personality traits symbolic of alienation as determinants of apostasy. Can the influence of the personality traits be explained by the earlier familial experiences and, if not, which serves as the more important determinant of apostasy? Table 3.9 shows the simultaneous effect of the quality of parental relations and the superindex of "alienation." To simplify the presentation, we have combined the medium-high and high categories on the superindex.

Table 3.9: The Joint Effects of Parental Relations and the Personality Predisposition Index on Apostasy in Each Religious Group (in percentages)

Predisposition Index	Quality of Parental Relations						
	Good		Fair		Poor		Difference
Jews							
Low	5	(671)	6	(344)	11	(125)	6
Medium	9	(293)	18	(225)	28	(141)	19
High	21	(84)	36	(98)	57	(75)	36
Difference	16		30		46		
Protestants							
Low	6	(5,349)	11	(2,210)	19	(619)	13
Medium	15	(1,313)	18	(796)	32	(305)	17
High	30	(186)	44	(166)	56	(108)	26
Difference	24		33		37		
Catholics							
Low	3	(1,937)	5	(842)	16	(289)	13
Medium	6	(566)	10	(329)	17	(165)	11
High	14	(109)	24	(76)	34	(57)	20
Difference	11		19		18		

The patterns of Table 3.9 are very much like those of 3.7. Instead of parental relations explaining away the impact of the personality attributes on apostasy, we see that both have independent effects and combine to increase apostasy. Among Jews and Protestants, it would appear that the personality syndrome of alienation has a somewhat stronger effect on apostasy than quality of parental relations (this can be seen by comparing the percentage differences in the rows and columns). Among Catholics, quality of parental relations is about as important as the personality syndrome. In any event, we now know that "alienation" is a determinant of apostasy independent of the quality of parental relations. Although poor parental relations may contribute to this trait, then do not fully account for it, nor do they explain the impact of "alienation" on apostasy.

Emerging from this analysis is a picture of the apostate as a person who is likely to be maladjusted in his social milieu, who is oriented to values that are not widely held in society (intellectuality, culture, and idealism) and who is highly critical of the societal status quo, that is, committed to radical social change. Although these traits seem to have their origin, at least in part, in poor childhood relations with parents, their connection with apostasy is largely independent of parental relations. On a higher level of abstraction, these traits appear to be indicators of alienation and rebellion. The alienated are apt to reject a religious identification on the grounds that religious institutions are part of the societal status quo that they reject. Those who have the apostasy germs identified in this chapter, especially the higher values, are also likely to be sensitive to empirically based truths and thus experience strain between religious belief and secular forces. Finally, these apostasy germs, again higher values in particular, also suggest sensitivity to the values of achievement and universalism, in contrast to the values of ascription and particularism. Thus, all three of the theories of apostasy described earlier find some support in these data, with the alienation-rebellion theory gaining most support.

This portrait of the apostate as committed to higher values, maladjusted, and leftist in political orientation, has much in common with the intellectual in American society.[6] We have already seen that the self-description "intellectual" most sharply differentiates apostates in all religions from identifiers. The connection between intellectualism and apostasy is examined in much more detail in the next chapter.

NOTES

1. There were three items that showed a difference of seven percentage points in one religious group but smaller differences in the same direction in the other two. "Athletic" differentiated *Catholic* apostates and identifiers by seven percentage points; "energetic" did so for Protestants; and "middlebrow" for Jews.

2. Melvin Seeman, *op, cit.,* and Russell Middleton, *op. cit.*

3. Gwynn Nettler, "A Measure of Alienation," *American Sociological Review,* December 1957, pp. 670-677.

4. The Gandhi movement in India is a notable exception.

5. This index was constructed by assigning a score of 1 to the "very liberal" response and a score of 1 to the very or fairly unconventional responses. Those who are high on radicalism scored 2 on this index, those who are medium scored 1 and those who are low scored 0.

6. The liberal, leftist bias of American intellectuals is discussed at length in Paul F. Lazarsfeld and Wagner Thielens, Jr., *The Academic Mind*, New York: Free Press, 1958.

Chapter 4

INTELLECTUALISM AND APOSTASY

The alleged incompatibility between intellectualism and religion has been the subject of much scholarly, literary, and journalistic treatment.[1] The argument for such incompatibility is based on the intellectual's commitment to empirically verifiable truths and his critical stance toward ideas in general and traditional beliefs in particular. On this basis, intellectuals are prone to question the validity of accepted religious beliefs. Since religiosity is an important foundation of religious identification, intellectuals should be especially prone to apostasy. We would also expect intellectuals to abandon a religious identity because of the weakness in this group of the other foundation of religious identity—communality or ethnicity. Committed to universalism-achievement values, intellectuals no doubt place less emphasis than do others on ties based on particularism and ascription.

The empirical evidence leaves little doubt of the presumed incompatibility. Thus, in the previous chapter, we saw that the self-description most strongly associated with apostasy was "intellectual." And other studies based on this same body of data[2] and on an earlier NORC study of graduate students[3] have demonstrated higher apostasy rates among the more intellectual students. These findings have touched off a debate in the literature about the meaning of the connection between intellectualism and apostasy. Using the data of the 1957 NORC study of graduate students, Rodney Stark argued for the fundamental incompatibility between religion and science, the latter being close to the concern of this chapter, intellectualism.[4] Using the same body of data, Joseph Zelan wrote a master's essay on apostasy and later published an article on it, advancing the novel thesis that intellectualism is a functional alternative to religion and as such constitutes a "new religion."[5] This argument was further developed by Zelan's senior colleague, Andrew Greeley of the NORC staff who took the position that apostasy leads to intellectualism rather than the other way around.[6]

This chapter serves several functions. First, the basic relationship between apostasy and intellectualism will be reexamined, using a more refined measure of intellectuality than that used in the other studies. Second, we shall try to interpret this relationship by considering what impact the known correlates of apostasy have on the connection between it and intellectualism. Can the relationship be explained away by such properties as neuroticism or radicalism that tend to be associated with both intellectuality and apostasy, or will the incompatibility persist when these other factors are taken into account? Third, we shall use data from a much more recent study of college professors[7] to see whether the social group toward which the intellectual college seniors are oriented also shows the strains toward apostasy. The final section of the chapter will examine the relative merits of Stark and Zelan-Greeley in their debate about the nature of the connection between apostasy and intellectualism.

Measuring Intellectuality

A good deal has been written about intellectuals, what they do, who they are, and what their role is in society.[8] It is generally conceded that intellectuals are concerned with truth and ideas in such areas as cognition (science, knowledge), aesthetics (art, beauty), and morality (ideology, philosophy, theology). They create, preserve, and transmit truths and ideas in these realms. If there is general agreement on the meaning of the concept of intellectual, how might one go about classifying people according to how intellectual they are? In the NORC study with which we are dealing, a number of indicators of intellectualism are to be found, and we have concentrated on those that relate to an occupational commitment to the intellectual life. In short, intellectualism will be measured by degree of commitment to an intellectual career.

The respondents were asked a series of questions dealing with occupational values, those attributes that they considered most important when selecting a career. Among these are two values that bear directly on intellectuality, "living and working in the world of ideas" and "opportunities to be original and creative." In addition to occupational values, we know the anticipated career of these college seniors, and those careers that require graduate (as distinct from professional) study, the physical, biological, and social sciences and the humanities, are also treated as signs of an intellectual commitment. Finally, we know the setting in which these college graduates expect eventually to be employed. Those who reported that they expected to work for colleges and universities, that is, those who were choosing the academic life, are also treated as manifesting a trait of an intellectual career commitment. To measure intellectuality or, more accurately, degree of commitment to an intellectual career, we have treated endorsement of both intellectual values as one dimension, a career in the humanities, physical or social sciences as a second dimension, and orientation toward academic employment as a third dimension. Possessing two or three of these traits qualifies the student as being high on career intellectuality. Those with one of these traits have been classified in the medium category and those without any fall into the low category. The majority of these college seniors were not intellectuals, as 60 percent of them failed to have any of these traits. Some 28 percent fell into the medium category, and only 12 percent scored high on career intellectuality. The Jews were somewhat more likely to be intellectually oriented than the other religions as 18 percent of them were in the high category compared with 12 percent of the Protestants and 10 percent of the Catholics.

Career Intellectuality and Apostasy

The relationship between career intellectuality and apostasy within each religion is shown in Table 4.1.

Table 4.1: Apostasy by Career Intellectuality (in percentages)

Career Intellectuality		Jews	Protestants	Catholics
High	(Score 2,3)	27 (638)	29 (2,153)	17 (811)
Medium	(Score 1)	14 (1,064)	14 (4,918)	9 (2,090)
Low	(Score 0)	8 (1,767)	8 (10,656)	5 (4,868)

In each religious group those who score high on career intellectuality are more than three times as likely to apostatize as those who score low. As in many other tables dealing with predispositions toward apostasy, the relationship is strongest among the Protestants and weakest among the Catholics, with the Jews resembling the Protestants in this instance. The strain toward incompatibility between intellectualism and religious identification, documented by others, is thus substantiated by these data. But it is important to note that, even among the most intellectually oriented in each religion, a majority do *not* apostatize. In short, most would-be intellectuals are able to integrate a religious identity with their intellectual commitment. Whether this becomes increasingly harder to do as these graduates become more socialized into intellectual careers is a matter of conjecture, but data will be presented later dealing with apostasy rates among college professors that suggest that this may indeed become more difficult over time.

It is of some value to compare the index of career intellectuality, which might be thought of as an objective measure, with the more subjective self-description as an intellectual discussed in the previous chapter. In each religion, somewhat more describe themselves as intellectuals than score high on career intellectuality and, although the two measures are related, the relationship is far from perfect. Only among Jews do a majority of those high on career intellectuality describe themselves as intellectuals (56 percent), compared with 41 percent of the Protestants and 46 percent of the Catholics in the high career-intellectuality category. At the other extreme we find some in each religion who consider themselves intellectuals even though they endorse none of the three intellectual career items. Among Jews low on career intellectuality, 16 percent consider themselves intellectuals; among Protestants the proportion is 10 percent; and among Catholics 12 percent. In short, a strong career commitment to an intellectual life is no guarantee that the student will think of himself as an intellectual, and some students do not hesitate to apply this label to themselves even though they are not oriented toward an intellectual career. The question arises as to whether these two measures of intellectuality affect apostasy. Table 4.2 provides the answer.

Table 4.2: Apostasy by Career Intellectuality and Self-Description as an Intellectual (in percentages)

		Career Intellectuality		
Self-Described Intellectuals		**High**	**Medium**	**Low**
Jews:	yes	32 (358)	19 (320)	13 (290)
	no	21 (280)	12 (744)	7 (1,477)
Protestants:	yes	35 (898)	22 (1,141)	15 (1,194)
	no	23 (1,255)	12 (3,777)	7 (9,462)
Catholics:	yes	20 (375)	14 (515)	7 (596)
	no	14 (436)	7 (1,575)	4 (4,272)

The subjective and objective measures each contribute to apostasy and their joint effect are additive. Thus, those who do not think of themselves as intellectuals but who are committed strongly to an intellectual career are more likely to apostatize than their counterparts without a commitment to an intellectual career, and conversely, on each level of career commitment, those who think of themselves as intellectuals are more likely to apostatize. This would suggest that the measure of intellectuality would be strengthened by including the subjective component as well, but we shall confine the analysis in this chapter to the objective index already described. Adding further indicators to it would only strengthen correlations but would not alter the pattern of results.

If there is a strain between intellectualism and a religious commitment, as the previous tables suggest, then we should find that even among the identifiers religiosity is weakened among the more intellectual students. As noted in the opening chapter, the respondents were asked to identify themselves on a five-point scale of religiosity from very religious to very nonreligious.[9] The very and fairly religious categories have been combined to indicate the religious students. In Chapter 1 we saw that the identity of the Jewish students rested much less on religiosity than did that of the Protestants and Catholics. For this reason we should find intellectualism especially undermining religiosity among Jewish identifiers. Where it does so among Protestants and Catholics, they are apt to cease being identifiers and become apostates. Table 4.3 shows that there is much merit

Table 4.3: Proportion of Religious Among Identifiers in Each Religion by Career Intellectuality (Identifiers Only), (in percentages)

Career Intellectuality	Jews	Protestants	Catholics
Low	49 (1,551)	79 (9,399)	91 (4,483)
Medium	44 (882)	76 (4,086)	89 (1,839)
High	30 (458)	70 (1,018)	87 (675)

to this reasoning. Among Jews, where communality plays a major role in identification, religiosity sharply declines as intellectualism increases. Among Protestants, where religiosity is much more important to identity, the fall-off is not nearly as sharp, but even here the pattern is found, and among Catholics, the group whose religious identity rests most on religious belief, the pattern is weakest but still evident. In short, even among identifiers, the strain between intellectualism and religion can be found.

The Impact of Intellectuality in the Light of the Other Correlates of Apostasy

The previous analysis has identified a number of factors that predispose people to apostasy. To what extent do these apostasy "germs" help explain the greater apostasy of the more intellectual students? Quality of parental relations proved to be a strong determinant of apostasy independent of the other factors uncovered so far. Could it be that intellectuals are prone to apostatize, not because of any incompatibility between their value commitments and their religious identification, but merely because those who lean toward intellectual endeavors are the very ones who experienced poor parental relations? This is not as far-fetched an idea as it might first seem. The intellectual path is not the common one for those who aspire to success in American society, as indicated by the small proportion of the sample opting for intellectual careers. That youth should choose this "deviant" path might well reflect troubles in the family of origin. By this logic it is poor parental relations that lead both to intellectualism and apostasy. Indeed, there is a connection between intellectuality and poor parental relations, for in each religious group the most intellectual students were twice as likely as the least intellectual students to report poor relations with parents. Whether quality of parental relations in any way explain the connection between apostasy and intellectualism is shown by Table 4.4.

Reading across the rows and down the columns we see that intellectuality and quality of parental relations independently

Table 4.4: Apostasy by Career Intellectuality and Quality of Parental Relations (in percentages)

Career Intellectuality	Parental Relations Good		Fair		Poor		Difference
Jews							
Low	6	(571)	5	(331)	15	(128)	9
Medium	8	(320)	19	(209)	25	(99)	17
High	12	(159)	28	(122)	48	(107)	36
Difference	6		23		33		
Protestants							
Low	6	(4,323)	10	(1,808)	18	(529)	12
Medium	9	(1,832)	16	(933)	25	(319)	16
High	21	(706)	27	(438)	51	(196)	30
Difference	15		17		33		
Catholics							
Low	3	(1,708)	5	(774)	12	(271)	9
Medium	5	(673)	9	(343)	22	(142)	17
High	14	(239)	17	(133)	29	(94)	15
Difference	1		12		17		

affect apostasy and that within each religious group they have an additive effect. At the same time there is some interaction between the two determinants as the impact of one predisposition is strongest when the other is present. This can be seen from the pattern of the percentage differences in the rows and columns in each sector of the table. In short, quality of parental relations does not explain why intellectualism is linked to apostasy. The thesis that there is a strain between the values held by intellectuals and the values underlying a religious identification survives this test.

The stereotype of the neurotic intellectual is quite common and finds support in the data on hand as the more intellectually oriented students were much more likely to be in the maladjusted category than the nonintellectually oriented. But, just as poor parental relations did not explain the connection between intellectualism and apostasy, neither does maladjustment. When career intellectuality and adjustment-maladjustment are considered simultaneously, the results are very much like those in Table 4.4. On every level of adjustment-maladjustment, those high on career intellectuality are more likley to apostatize than those who are low, and when career intellectuality is held constant, adjustment-maladjustment continues to be related to apostasy. These findings hold for each religion.

A radical political orientation, which was strongly related to apostasy, is also more characteristic of the highly intellectual students. In each religion, the stronger the commitment to intellectualism, the greater the radicalism. But radicalism by no means explains the association between intellectualism and apostasy, as can be seen from Table 4.5.

Table 4.5: Apostasy by Career Intellectuality and Radicalism (in percentages)

Career Intellectuality	Radicalism: Low		Medium		High		Difference
Jews							
Low	5	(1,039)	10	(525)	19	(149)	14
Medium	7	(485)	18	(401)	29	(151)	22
High	15	(192)	28	(267)	40	(172)	25
Difference	10		18		21		
Protestants							
Low	5	(7,716)	16	(2,407)	33	(215)	28
Medium	7	(3,010)	24	(1,571)	45	(218)	38
High	14	(931)	35	(989)	57	(202)	43
Difference	9		19		24		
Catholics							
Low	3	(3,267)	7	(1,277)	14	(176)	11
Medium	4	(1,185)	14	(715)	24	(133)	20
High	8	(353)	20	(357)	42	(84)	34
Difference	5		13		28		

Reading down the columns within each religion, we find apostasy steadily increasing with career intellectuality. Again there are interaction effects, with the relationship strongest among the most radical. A comparison of the column and row percentage differences indicates that radicalism is an even stronger determinant of apostasy than intellectuality. Taken together, these attributes account for a good deal of the variation in apostasy within each religion.

The remaining apostasy germ, what we have called commitment to higher values, is so close to intellectuality as to be almost tautological. After all, describing oneself as "intellectual" is one of the higher values. It is, therefore, not surprising that these two indices are highly correlated and when their joint impact on apostasy is considered, we find that career intellectuality largely washes out the connection between higher values and apostasy. Presumably, it is what higher values shares with career intellectuality that leads it to its effect on apostasy.

So far, we have considered intellectuality in combination with but a single other predisposition toward apostasy. A more rigorous test of the independence of intellectuality would be to consider it in the context of all the other "germs" simultaneously. We have seen that career intellectuality is related to parental relations, maladjustment, radicalism, and higher values. To show the impact of intellectuality alone, when these other factors are taken into account, we have made a predisposition index of the other four determinants. It is hardly surprising that intellectualism is strongly related to this predisposition index. Among Jews, 72 percent of the most intellectually oriented have at least one other "germ," among Protestants, this is true of 54 percent and among Catholics, of 63 percent. At the other extreme, 40 percent of the nonintellectual Jews have at least one of the four germs, compared with 25 percent of the nonintellectual Protestants and 29 percent of the nonintellectual Catholics. Given this strong relationship between career intellectuality and the other determinants of apostasy, will career intellectuality still relate to apostasy when the other determinants are held roughly constant? Table 4.6 provides the answer. (The base figures in this table are reduced because we are including parental relations which was measured only in the fourth wave.

The predisposition index in this table was developed by giving a score of 1 to each of the previously examined "germs," poor parental relations, maladjustment, radicalism, and higher values. The columns show that intellectualism is still related to apostasy when these other factors are taken into account. Of course, the predisposition index shows a much stronger relationship to apostasy than does intellectuality (compare the row and column percentage differences) but this is hardly surprising for

Table 4.6: Apostasy by Career Intellectuality by Four-Item Predisposition Index (in percentages)

Career Intellectuality	Low (0)		Medium (1)		High (2-4)		Difference
Jews							
Low	3	(609)	8	(291)	25	(110)	22
Medium	8	(276)	14	(220)	31	(121)	23
High	8	(111)	22	(116)	42	(160)	34
Difference	5		15		17		
Protestants							
Low	6	(4,943)	12	(1,317)	33	(245)	27
Medium	8	(1,872)	18	(879)	32	(275)	24
High	18	(615)	30	(475)	49	(234)	31
Difference	12		18		16		
Catholics							
Low	3	(1,914)	8	(629)	15	(149)	12
Medium	5	(653)	9	(357)	22	(126)	17
High	1	(163)	19	(171)	27	(122)	16
Difference	8		11		12		

it is made up of four "germs." The critical point is that intellectuality is still related to apostasy even when the other "germs" are taken into account. Moreover, there is little point of conceiving of intellectualism in abstraction from the other traits, for they tend to coalesce in the kinds of persons who are oriented toward intellectual careers. In sum, the import of this analysis is that intellectuality is indeed a "determinant" of apostasy; intellectuals do experience some difficulty incorporating a religious identity with the other components of their self-image and their values. This is not to say that the difficulty is insurmountable. On the contrary, the great majority of the intellectuals in each religion do retain a religious identity. Nonetheless, the commitment to empirically based ideas and to universalism-achievement norms characteristic of intellectuals does tend to undermine religious identification.

The Cumulative Effect of the Predisposition Factors on Apostasy

Some five traits have now been identified as predisposing college seniors to apostasy. It is of some interest to consider the cumulative effect of these factors on apostasy within each religion. Table 4.7 shows how an index composed of these five traits relates to apostasy.

Table 4.7: Apostasy by Number of Predisposing Traits (in percentages)

Number of Predisposing Traits	Jews		Protestants		Catholics	
5	[80]	(5)	[85]	(7)	[67]	(9)
4	52	(52)	63	(51)	32	(31)
3	38	(150)	45	(261)	24	(125)
2	24	(300)	29	(910)	16	(404)
1	10	(622)	15	(2,811)	9	(1,149)
0	5	(885)	7	(6,815)	3	(2,567)

The number of students in each religion with all five traits is too small to yield reliable percentages and for this reason the percentages are bracketed. Nonetheless, the overall pattern is quite marked. These five traits in combination account for much of the variance in apostasy in each religion. More than half of the Jews and Protestants who have at least four of these traits apostatize. (Among Catholics a majority is reached only among the tiny number who have all five traits.) By reading across each row we find that, for any given number of traits, Protestants are most likely to apostatize and Catholics are least likely to, with Jews in between.

Faculty Apostasy

The measure of intellectualism used in this chapter deals with commitment to an intellectual career. Although intellectuals support themselves in many ways—as free-lance writers, as editors of magazines, and as artists living off their creations—the archetypical home of the intellectual is the university, and one of the elements in the index is whether the student anticipates being employed in a college or university. The academic culture, perhaps more than any other, is committed to universalism-achievement values. Moreover, academics have a commitment to empirically verifiable truths and to questioning traditional values. Hence, the strains on a religious identity based in part on traditional beliefs and in part on ascription should be particularly strong in the academic setting. From this point of view, the college seniors that we have classified as intellectually oriented might be presumed to be undergoing what Merton has identified as *anticipatory socialization,* the process whereby people begin to take on the values of the groups they hope to join.[10] But what if these would-be intellectuals have misread the situation and true intellectuals have no difficulty retaining their religious identification? Were this the case, then the theories advanced to account for apostasy would be wrong.

Fortunately, data are available from other studies that permit us to examine the extent of apostasy among college professors in America. In 1969, the Carnegie Foundation, in collaboration with the American Council on Education, carried out a massive survey of college students and college teachers. In addition, a survey of students and faculty members was carried out at Columbia University immediately following the troubles that erupted on that campus in the spring of 1968. As a sign of the institutionalization of the NORC invention, both of these studies included the two questions on religion that make the study of apostasy possible.

Faculty rates of apostasy, as measured in 1969, are, in each religion, substantially higher than those of college seniors in 1961. Thus, among Jewish professors 28 percent were apostates in 1969; among Protestant professors 24 percent were apostates, and the Catholic professors showed the same rate as the Protestants, 24 percent. These rates are quite comparable to those found for the most intellectual students as reported in Table 4.2. The Jewish faculty rate exceeded the highly intellectual Jewish rate by only one percentage point. Among Catholics, the faculty rate exceeded the rate among the highly intellectual students by 7 percentage points, and only among the Protestants did the highly intellectual students of 1961 exceed the faculty apostasy rate (29 percent compared with 24 percent).

Of course, not all academics at American colleges and universities think of themselves as intellectuals or fit the mold of this social type.[11] One way of purifying the classification of faculty members in this respect is to take into account the quality of the school at which they are located. Academics at high-quality institutions are no doubt expected to be more intellectual, and they undoubtedly publish more than academics at low-quality schools. If there is a fundamental strain between intellectualism and a religious identity, apostasy among faculty members should increase with the quality of their school. Table 4.8, based on the 1969 Carnegie study, shows this to be so.

Table 4.8: Faculty Apostasy by Quality of School (in percentages)

Quality of Teaching Institution	Religion of Origin: Jewish	Protestant	Catholic
Low	25 (942)	18 (12,176)	18 (3,125)
Medium	30 (1,952)	24 (12,228)	22 (3,043)
High	31 (2,757)	34 (10,206)	34 (2,219)

In each religious group, faculty apostasy increases with quality of school, which might be considered a crude measure of intellectualism. At the high-quality schools, the apostasy rates in each religion reach at least 30 percent, figures that are even higher than those found for the most intellectually oriented seniors (see Table 4.2). The impact of school quality is largest among the Protestants and Catholics and smallest among the Jewish professors. Although the measures of intellectualism in the faculty and student samples are quite different, there is some merit in comparing apostasy in the two groups when intellectualism is taken into account. A comparison of Table 4.2 and 4.8 shows that in each religion the faculty apostasy rates exceed those of the college seniors. The gap between faculty apostasy and student apostasy is narrowest for the most intellectually oriented Jewish and Protestant students when compared with professors of their religion of origin at high-quality schools; for Catholics, the gap is substantial on each level of intellectuality. It is hardly surprising that faculty at low- and medium-quality schools are much more likely to apostatize than students of a moderate or low intellectual orientation, for even the poorest universities and colleges still belong within the parameters of the intellectual community. But a comparison of Tables 4.1 and 4.8 shows that faculty at high-quality schools are more prone to apostasy than the most intellectually oriented students. The latter are indeed taking on the coloring of the occupational group to which they aspire and, in fact, they still have some way to go before they match the apostasy of academics in high-quality institutions.

This conclusion becomes even more evident when we focus on one of the great universities in the country, Columbia. The 1968 survey of the Bureau of Applied Social Research found faculty apostasy rates in each religion far greater than those in high-quality universities generally. Among those of the Columbia faculty raised as Jews, only 58 percent continued to identify themselves with the Jewish religion, 5 percent had converted to some other religion, and 37 percent were apostates. Adherence to the religion of origin was even lower for the Protestants and Catholics on the Columbia faculty. Only 40 percent of those raised as Protestants continued to think of themselves as Protestants, 9 percent had converted to some other religion, and 51 percent were apostates. Among those at Columbia raised as Catholics, 50 percent continued to identify with Catholicism, 8 percent were converts, and 42 percent were apostates. As these data indicate, apostasy rates at a major institution of higher learning are so substantial that the phenomenon is no longer the position of a small minority. In a truly intellectual climate, such as Columbia University, the chances of apostasy move toward 50-50.

The Cause-Effect Debate: Stark vs. Zelan and Greeley

As noted at the outset of the chapter, the repeatedly observed connection between apostasy and intellectualism has touched off a controversy about the causal direction of this relationship. What is so fascinating about this debate is that the debators draw largely upon the same body of data. On one side is Rodney Stark who makes use of the 1957 NORC survey of graduate students (the survey that will be forever remembered as the origin of the two religious questions that make the study of apostasy possible) to argue that intellectualism undermines a religious commitment.[12] The proponents of the opposing view are two sociologists associated with NORC, Joseph Zelan, who used the same 1957 survey to write a Master's essay about apostasy and who, in 1968, published a paper based on his Master's essay,[13] and Andrew Greeley, whose dissertation about religion and career choice[14] was based on the same 1961 NORC survey that is under analysis in this book. According to Zelan and Greeley, there is no fundamental strain between religion and intellectualism. However, those who, for one reason or another, relinquish their religious identity are attracted to the intellectual life because it offers some of the comforts lost by giving up religion. To Zelan and Greeley it is apostasy that leads to intellectuality rather than the other way around, as Stark argues. Whether one treats apostasy as a cause or as an effect of intellectualism can be gleaned from the manner in which the supporting data are presented. Those who view intellectualism as a cause treat apostasy as the *dependent* variable and show apostasy rates for those with varying degrees of commitment to the intellectual life. Conversely, those who think that apostasy causes intellectualism compare apostates and identifiers with respect to their intellectual orientations. As can be seen from the way in which the tables of this chapter have been percentaged, Stark is not alone in his battle with Zelan and Greeley for we too assume some strain between intellectualism and a religious identification and treat intellectualism as a cause of apostasy.

Stark, Caplovitz, and Sherrow have the advantage of offering the more simple explanation of the correlation between intellectualism and apostasy and thus have William of Occam on their side. Ours is the more simple explanation, for we are able to locate within the concept of intellectualism components of incompatibility with a religious commitment. Zelan and Greeley, in contrast, refuse to recognize any strain between intellectuality and religion, and thus they must come to grips with two problems which complicate their casual model. First, why should apostasy lead to intellectualism, and second, if apostasy is not caused by intellectualism, what does cause apostasy? The weakness of the Zelan-Greeley argument rests not so much on their view of the causes of apostasy, although by ruling out intellectualism, their theory of apostasy must necessarily be incomplete. Rather, it lies in their assumption of a causal connection between apostasy and intellectualism. Zelan and Greeley postulate certain functions of religious belief, mainly providing meaning to the world and one's place in it and hence alleviating the anxiety and stress of the person who does not have ready answers to life's fundamental questions. According to their theory, some global concept of "alienation," whether caused by an unhappy home, discovery of drugs, radicalism, or whatever, jars certain people loose from their religious moorings, setting them adrift on the seas of life. Overcome by uncertainty, anxiety, and meaninglessness, they drift toward intellectualism, which presumably provides them with new answers to alleviate their anxieties.

To support this view of the causal chain, Zelan and Greeley present two kinds of evidence. First, they show that the apostates are more miserable than the identifiers, presumably because they have lost a ready answer to the meaning of life. Second, they try to show that the apostates are more likely to be attracted to the intellectual life as a "new religion" to relieve their suffering. A critical third link in this causal chain is hardly dealt with at all by Zelan and Greeley: whether the apostates who turn to intellectualism have their suffering eased by their "new religion." Each of these links in the Zelan-Greeley causal chain will be subjected to close examination on the basis of the same data used by Greeley—the 1961 NORC panel study of college seniors.

THE CONNECTION BETWEEN APOSTASY AND UNHAPPINESS

Central to the Zelan-Greeley argument is the finding presented in the last chapter, that apostates are not as likely to describe themselves as happy as the identifiers. This finding is taken as confirmation of the first link in their causal chain, namely that those who willy-nilly relinquish religion pay the price of unhappiness. But Zelan-Greeley are not content to rest their case on this aggregate correlation. Borrowing from reference-group theory,[15] they hypothesize that apostates who are most deviant from their group of origin should be the ones who suffer the most. Since Catholics have a much lower apostasy rate than Protestants or Jews, they reason that the gap in happiness between apostates and identifiers is greater among Catholics than in the other religions. Both Greeley, on the basis of the 1961 survey, and Zelan, on the basis of the 1957 survey, present data purportedly supporting this thesis. They present tables showing that the discrepancy in happiness (Greeley) and morale (Zelan) between apostates and identifiers is greater among Catholics than among Jews and Protestants. Their tables show that the Catholic apostates are particularly unhappy, presumably because they are even more deviant relative to their group of origin than the Jewish and Protestant apostates. However plausible this reasoning, the Greeley argument, at least, is wrong for the simple reason that his data are in error. His Table 8.8 (p. 192 of *Religion and Career*) shows that the greatest discrepancy in unhappiness occurs among the Catholics because, according to his figures, 80 percent of the Catholic apostates fail to describe themselves as happy compared with only 42 percent of the Catholic identifiers, a percentage difference of 38 points (far exceeding the comparable difference among Protestants and Jews). But the same finding is reported in Table 3.1 of the previous chapter of this book, and, although we report the percentage of happy rather than of unhappy respondents, the critical contradiction is to be found in the third column of our Table 3.1 where the discrepancy between Catholic identifiers and apostates on happiness is 18 percentage points, not 38 percentage points, and, in this respect, the Catholics are not different from the Jews or Protestants. In fact, our data show that the Jewish apostates are even less likely than the Catholic ones to describe themselves as happy. How is it possible that such different results arise from the same set of data? The answer, we suspect, lies in the different technologies utilized for data analysis. In Greeley's day, the computer was not yet a part of the sociologist's standard equipment and, to make this survey amenable to the more primitive equipment of the time, Greeley dealt with a 10 percent sample, whereas we have dealt with all the cases. Second, the counter sorter (if that is what Greeley used) is always vulnerable to human error. Whatever the reasons, the fact remains that the Greeley thesis for the causal connection between apostasy and intellectualism rests in part on faulty data.

Greeley's error is compounded by another set of false data, his findings on the difference between apostates and identifiers in the different religions with regard to their readiness to describe themselves as intellectuals. The logic of his reference-group argument leads him to predict that Catholic apostates will be particularly drawn to intellectualism because they are most in need of a substitute religion and that the gap in the frequency of self-identified intellectuals among apostates and identifiers will be greatest for the Catholics. The error in this instance is that only 35 percent of the Catholic apostates described themselves as intellectuals, not 47 percent as Greeley reports. As a result, Jewish apostates, who presumably need a substitute religion least, have the highest rate of self-defined intellectuals, and the gap between Catholic apostates and identifiers is no larger (in fact, it is smaller) than in the other religions.[16]

The logic of the Zelan-Greeley argument fares somewhat better with Zelan's data. Zelan develops a two-item index of morale and in his Table 5, he shows that the Catholic apostates in this sample of graduate students are most likely to have low morale (57 percent compared with 52 percent for Jewish apostates and 44 percent for Protestant apostates). Moreover, his Catholic apostates compared with Catholic identifiers are especially drawn to the self-description "intellectual" in keeping with their notion that Catholic apostates in particular need a substitute religion.

THE CONNECTION BETWEEN APOSTASY AND INTELLECTUALISM

Whether the assumption, derived from reference-group theory, that Catholic apostates will suffer the most and hence will be most driven to a substitute religion is correct (Zelan's data) or incorrect (Greeley's data) is not too material to the main issue, the causal direction of the relationship between apostasy and intellectualism. As noted, the Zelan-Greeley thesis is that apostates turn to intellectualism as a substitute religion. For apostates, intellectualism provides the answers that were formerly provided by religion and, hence, their anxieties are reduced by their "new religion." The data to test this thesis were available to both Greeley and Zelan, but, incredibly enough, neither of them presents the critical table, a table showing the relationship between happiness or morale and apostasy among those who did find a new religion (intellectualism) and those who did not. Zelan does make some attempt to confront this issue, but, instead of using the self-description "intellectual," he uses a more indirect indicator of an intellectual home, whether or not the graduate student is currently attending an elite university. In his Table 6, Zelan shows that Jewish apostates at elite colleges are somewhat less likely to have low morale than Jewish indentifiers (48 percent compared with 56 percent, hardly a large difference), a pattern that also holds for the Protestants (36 percent compared with 46 percent). But the group of apostates most in need of a substitute religion according to Greeley and Zelan—the Catholics—show the opposite pattern. The Catholic apostates attending elite schools tend to have the lowest morale (68 percent) compared with Catholic identifiers in presumably less intellectual environments (53 percent). Thus, the only test related to the substitute-religion hypothesis to be found in the work of Zelan and Greeley (Zelan's Table 6) provides what at best can be described as an ambiguous picture.

The more direct test that both Zelan and Greeley could have made of their hypothesis, but chose not to, involves the self-description "happy" as a benefit of the new religion. If intellectualism is indeed a religious substitute, performing the functions of reassurance of organized religion, then we should find that the apostates who have chosen the intellectual way of life should be less disturbed and more happy than those who have not. Although we can use the single item the self-description "intellectual" for this test, we shall use the stronger measure of intellectual commitment, the three-category index of career intellectualism developed earlier. Table 4.9 reports the percentage of apostates and identifiers on each level of intellectuality who describe themselves as "happy." (This is done for each religion.)

Table 4.9: Respondents Choosing Self-Description "Happy" by Intellectualism Presented Separately for Apostates and Identifiers in Each Religion (in percentages)

	Career Intellectuality		
	Low	Medium	High
Jews			
Apostates	30 (135)	24 (148)	24 (172)
Identifiers	42 (1,632)	42 (916)	27 (466)
Protestants			
Apostates	36 (862)	35 (862)	25 (599)
Identifiers	54 (9,794)	53 (4,225)	45 (1,553)
Catholics			
Apostates	32 (223)	32 (187)	18 (135)
Identifiers	47 (4,645)	45 (1,903)	40 (676)

By reading across the rows, we see that commitment to intellectualism results in less happiness for identifiers and apostates alike in each religion. The group most in need of a substitute religion to relieve its anxieties, the Catholic apostates, are much less likely to find happiness in intellectualism than their peers who do not turn to the intellectual world. Thus, only 18 percent of the highly intellectual Catholic apostates describe themselves as happy, compared with 32 percent of the Catholic apostates who score low on intellectualism. In fact, instead of being an antidote to unhappiness as the Zelan-Greeley substitute religion theory would hold, intellectualism turns out to be negatively related to happiness. Both apostasy and intellectualism seem to be causes of unhappiness, working in the same, rather than opposite, directions.

An even more powerful test is available. Instead of the single item "happy," we can use the index of adjustment-maladjustment, composed of a number of items. If intellectualism is indeed a substitute religion allaying fears and anxieties, then we should find that the most intellectual students are least likely to be maladjusted. Table 4.10 shows that this is clearly not the case.

Table 4.10: Respondents Maladjusted by Intellectualism Presented Separately for Apostates and Identifiers in Each Religion (in percentages)

	Career Intellectuality					
	Low		Medium		High	
Jews						
Apostates	33	(135)	38	(148)	40	(172)
Identifiers	15	(1,632)	17	(916)	25	(466)
Protestants						
Apostates	20	(862)	23	(693)	34	(599)
Identifiers	8	(9,794)	10	(4,225)	17	(1,553)
Catholics						
Apostates	22	(223)	26	(187)	39	(135)
Identifiers	10	(4,645)	14	(1,930)	22	(676)

We find much the same patterns as in the previous table. As intellectualism increases, apostates and identifiers alike are more likely to be maladjusted. Clearly, intellectualism is not serving the functions of a substitute religion attributed to it by Zelan and Greeley. Rather than reducing anxiety or maladjustment, it would seem that intellectualism reinforces these neurotic symptoms.

Tables 4.9 and 4.10 thus support Stark's and our view of the causal connection between intellectualism and apostasy. Intellectualism contains elements that place a strain on a religious identity. For some, this strain is so great that they give up their religion; for many others, it means a reduction in the degree of identification with a religion. As we saw earlier, intellectuals who do retain a religious identity are more likely to claim they are not religious. If anything, intellectualism and the sensitivity and awareness associated with it may well be a cause of "unhappiness" rather than unhappiness being the reason for choosing an intellectual way of life. Apart from its greater adherence to the dictum of Occam's razor, our view of the relationship eliminates the taint of antiintellectualism that creeps into the Zelan-Greeley view. In their view, apostates turn to intellectuality for the negative reason of avoiding pain, not because of any positive attraction to the values of truth, beauty, science, and culture embodied in the concept of intellectualism.

In sum, the thesis of this chapter, amply supported by the data, is that there is a strain between commitment to intellectualism and commitment to religion and that the former tends to undermine the latter. The intellectuals are apt to manifest all three processes undermining a religious identification. Thus, they are committed to empirically based truths and suspicious of nonempirical "truths" that form the bases of religion (the secularization theory); they are apt to be alienated from the dominant values of society in that they view themselves as unconventional and very liberal, committed to higher values rather than to materialism, and tending to the symptoms of maladjustment; and, finally, they are more committed than most people to the values of universalism and achievement which are in opposition to positions based on the values of ascription and particularism, as is the case of religion. These attributes of intellectuals do not stem from relinquishing a religious identity as Greeley and Zelan would have us believe, but rather they cause the shedding of a religious identity.

NOTES

1. See for example, A. D. White, *A History of the Warfares of Science with Theology and Christendom,* New York: Dover, 1960; and the writings of Bertrand Russell and Hans Reichenbach.

2. Andrew Greeley, *Religion and Career,* New York: Sheed and Ward, 1963, Ch. 8.

3. The earlier NORC study dealt with the finances of graduate students. See James Davis, *Stipends and Spouses,* Chicago: University of Chicago Press, 1962. The Davis study has achieved some immortality because it invented the two questions on religion that made possible the study of apostasy.

4. Rodney Stark, "On the Incompatibility of Religion and Science: A Survey of American Graduate Students," *Journal for the Scientific Study of Religion,* III, Fall, 1963.

5. Joseph Zelan, "Correlates of Religious Apostasy," unpublished master's essay, University of Chicago, 1960; and Zelan, "Religious Apostasy, Higher Education and Occupational Choice," *Sociology of Education,* Vol. 41, No. 4, Fall, 1968.

6. See Greeley, op cit. Also Greeley, "Comment on Stark's 'On the Incompatibility of Religion and Science,'" *Journal for the Scientific Study of Religion,* III, Spring, 1964, in which Greeley cites the data of Zelan's master's thesis.

7. These data are from the 1969 survey of college professors carried out by the American Council on Education on behalf of the Carnegie Foundation, henceforth known as the Carnegie study.

8. For a recent publication on this topic, see Charles Kadushin, *The American Intellectual Elite,* Boston: Little, Brown, 1974.

9. The role of religiosity in apostasy is examined more closely in the next chapter.

10. See Robert K. Merton and Alice Kitt Rossi, "Contributions to the Theory of Reference Group Behavior," in R.K. Merton and P.F. Lazarsfeld, eds., *Continuities in Social Research: Studies in the Scope and Method of "The American Soldier,"* New York: Free Press, 1960.

11. Among all professors, only 18 percent strongly agree with the statement, "I consider myself an intellectual," and 51 percent agree with reservations, bringing the total in these two categories to 70 percent. In short, 30 percent of all academics reject even the qualified label of intellectual.

12. Stark, op. cit.

13. Zelan, op. cit.

14. Greeley, op. cit.

15. R. K. Merton and Alice Kitt Rossi, op. cit.

16. The discrepancies can be explained by sampling error (the accidental poor luck of the 10 percent sample not being representative of the whole), human error (the misreading of counters), or perhaps need perception, a psychological theory that holds that people perceive what they want to perceive. We suspect that, of these possibilities, sampling error is most to blame. It is one thing to make inferences from the subsample marginals to the larger sample, and quite another to examine three variables simultaneously, for the simple reason that the case base becomes smaller. Greeley has only 48 Catholic apostates and 31 Jewish apostates in his subsample.

17. op. cit.

Chapter 5

RELIGIOSITY AND APOSTASY

MICHIGAN
CHRISTIAN
COLLEGE
LIBRARY
ROCHESTER, MICH.

From the outset, we have viewed religious identification as encompassing two components: religiosity, consisting of religious belief and ritual observance, and communality, identifying oneself with a social group. Having located a number of correlates of apostasy that appear to be determinants of it, we now examine the role of religiosity in the equation of apostasy. Is the loss of religious faith sufficient to produce apostasy? We saw in Chapter 1 that relatively few of the apostates raised in any religion consider themselves to be religious persons, but it does not necessarily follow that all who have lost faith become apostates. Secondly, do the various determinants of apostasy have their effect by undermining religious belief? This would seem plausible if religiosity were the only component of identification. By examining the role of religious faith, we shall be in a better position to assess the meaning of religious identification and its obverse, apostasy.

In the fourth wave of the NORC study conducted in 1964, there were several questions about religiosity, including frequency of church attendance. But in the first wave, which concerns us here, there was only a single question relating to religious commitment. All the seniors were asked to indicate how religious they were on a five-point scale: very religious, fairly religious, neither religious nor nonreligious, fairly nonreligious, or very nonreligious. For the purposes of this analysis, the religion scale is reduced to three categories: the religious (very or fairly), those who were neither or indifferent, and the nonreligious (very or fairly). In keeping with the findings of numerous other studies, the data show that religiosity is strongest among the Catholics and weakest among the Jews. Thus, 84 percent of the Catholics describe themselves as very religious, and only 9 percent say they are nonreligious; among Protestants, these figures are 69 percent and 17 percent; and among Jews, 39 percent and 40 percent. Among Jews, nonreligiosity is just as common as religiosity.

Table 1.2 showed that apostasy and religiosity are negatively related, but that table compared the religiosity of identifiers and apostates. Table 5.1 treats religiosity as a determinant of apostasy, showing apostasy rates in each religion according to strength of religious commitment.

Table 5.1: Apostasy by Religiosity (in percentages)

Religiosity	Jews	Protestants	Catholics
Religious	2 (1,379)	2 (12,515)	1 (6,620)
Neither/indifferent	7 (717)	20 (2,488)	27 (572)
Nonreligious	28 (1,404)	49 (2,979)	52 (668)

It comes as no surprise that in each religious group there is a strong relationship between apostasy and religious commitment. Hardly any of the religious seniors apostatize, and the largest proportions of apostates are found among the nonreligious. But of more interest is the fact the relationship is not nearly as strong among the Jews as among the Christians, as far fewer of the nonreligious Jews apostatize than nonreligious Protestants and Catholics. This is further evidence that the religious component is not as important for Jewish identification as it is for Protestant and Catholic identification. Table 5.1 tells us something else. Even among the nonreligious Christians, there are many—approximately half—who manage to retain their religious identity. The communal component is thus also important for Protestant and Catholic identity, its significance being more evident in this table than in Table 1.2, where the same data were percentaged in the other direction. While religiosity would appear to be a sufficient condition for maintaining an identification with the religious group, its absence is clearly *not* a sufficient condition for apostasy. Loss of faith may be a necessary condition for apostasy, but presumably other factors must be present before a break with the religious community occurs. Thus, the first question raised at the beginning of this chapter must be answered in the negative: Loss of faith by itself is no guarantee of apostasy.

Still to be considered is the relationship between the apostasy-provoking forces and religiosity. Do the various correlates of apostasy show similar relationships with religiosity and can the relationships established in the previous chapters be explained by loss of faith?

Religiosity, Parental Relations, and Apostasy

In Chapter 2 we saw that apostasy was strongly affected by the quality of relations with parents during childhood, a finding in keeping with the rebellion hypothesis of apostasy. By the same token, we can expect poor parental relations would result in rejecting religious beliefs held by parents. The data on hand show this to be so. In each religion, the percentage of respondents who are nonreligious increases as quality of parental relations declines. Among Jews, the increase is from 33 to 54 percent; among Protestants, from 13 to 28 percent; and among Catholics, from 6 to 19 percent. Given the significance of parental relations for religiosity, the question arises as to whether religiosity will explain the link between parental relations and apostasy. Table 5.2, which shows the joint effect of parental relations and religiosity on apostasy, provides the answer.

Table 5.2: Apostasy by Parental Relations and Religiosity (in percentages)

	Parental Relations					
	Good		Fair		Poor	
Jews						
Religious	2	(481)	0.4	(234)	4	(79)
Indifferent	5	(230)	10	(116)	13	(78)
Nonreligious	17	(347)	25	(323)	46	(183)
Protestants						
Religious	1	(5,145)	2	(2,130)	5	(596)
Indifferent	17	(894)	21	(433)	36	(159)
Nonreligious	41	(904)	51	(652)	66	(289)
Catholics						
Religious	1	(2,348)	0.4	(1,057)	3	(365)
Indifferent	24	(162)	26	(102)	33	(54)
Nonreligious	45	(138)	58	(106)	66	(95)

Although religiosity is related to the quality of parental relations, this fact does *not* explain the connection between parental relations and apostasy. Thus, on each level of religiosity in each religious group, apostasy increases as parental relations shift from good to poor. (This is shown in the rows of Table 5.2.) The patterns in the columns are equally significant. Apostasy, of course, increases as religiosity declines in each religion, but quality of parental relations has a profound effect on this relationship. Where parental relations are good, loss of faith is not nearly as likely to lead to apostasy as where parental relations are bad. Thus, the percentage differences increase sharply as quality of parental relations declines. There are other findings of interest in Table 5.2. In particular, Jews who are not religious but who have good relations with their parents are not nearly as likely to apostatize as their counterparts among the Protestants and Catholics (17 percent compared with 41 and 45 percent). This is yet another indication of the greater importance of communality for Jewish identification and, conversely, the greater importance of religiosity for the identification of Christians.

The fact that religiosity does not explain the connection between parental relations and apostasy reaffirms our earlier thesis that the family is important to the communal, as well as to the religious, component of identity. This is evident even when we consider the clearly religious students. Although relatively few of them apostatize, their apostasy rate nonetheless increases as relations with parents deteriorate. Thus, even among the religious college seniors, there is some tendency to disassociate with the religious community of origin when parental relations have been experienced as unpleasant. Clearly, this pattern is not due to loss of religious faith; it can only mean that the communal tie to the religious group has been undermined.

Personality Attributes, Religiosity, and Apostasy

In chapters 3 and 4, we identified four personality traits or value-orientations that were related to apostasy—emotional disturbance as opposed to social adjustment, commitment to higher values, a radical political perspective that involves rejection of the status quo, and an orientation to intellectualism and an intellectual career. The question now arises as to whether these determinants of apostasy have their effect by undermining religiosity, or whether they lead to apostasy independent of religiosity. That religiosity may indeed be the intervening variable is suggested by the fact that, in every instance, these symptoms of apostasy are associated with a decline of religious commitment. This can be seen from Table 5.3.

By reading down each column of Table 5.3, we find that the nonreligious in each religious group increase as the trait associated with apostasy increases. To be sure, differences appear among the traits. "Higher values" shows a fairly weak relationship to religiosity, as does adjustment-maladjustment. Radicalism, in contrast, shows the strongest relationship, closely followed by intellectualism. These differences parallel the significance of these traits for apostasy.

Table 5.3: Proportion Nonreligious According to the Symptoms of Apostasy: Adjustment-Maladjustment, Higher Values, Radicalism, and Intellectual Orientation (in percentages)

	Jews	Protestants	Catholics
Adjustment-Maladjustment			
Adjusted	33 (1,473)	12 (10,420)	6 (4,132)
Mixed	41 (1,416)	19 (6,240)	10 (2,882)
Maladjusted	54 (706)	31 (2,180)	18 (1,090)
Higher Values			
Low	35 (1,383)	14 (9,715)	7 (3,990)
Medium	41 (1,197)	18 (5,527)	10 (2,498)
High	47 (968)	24 (2,934)	12 (1,465)
Radicalism			
Low	29 (1,792)	10 (12,292)	4 (5,019)
Medium	49 (1,242)	29 (5,443)	16 (2,488)
High	61 (505)	44 (730)	22 (422)
Intellectualism			
Low	35 (1,706)	13 (10,339)	7 (4,747)
Medium	41 (1,043)	19 (4,821)	11 (2,045)
High	58 (638)	30 (2,151)	18 (810)

Having established that the traits associated with apostasy are also connected with loss of religious faith, we must now consider whether religiosity explains the effect of these traits on apostasy. As the data to be presented make clear, religiosity does *not* explain the connection. To be sure, the religious retain their identification whatever their position on the traits of apostasy (although even among the religious, apostasy increases slightly if the apostasy-provoking trait is present). But among the religiously indifferent and the nonreligious, the appearance of apostasy is very much linked to the presence of the traits of apostasy. Table 5.4 shows these results for adjustment-maladjustment. This table is limited to the religiously indifferent and the nonreligious, that is, those who lack the sufficient condition of religiosity for identification.

By reading down the columns of Table 5.4, we find, with one exception, that apostasy increases as we move from adjusted to maladjusted students. The one exception occurs among the religiously indifferent Catholics. In this group of Catholics, adjustment is not related to apostasy, indicating that their

Table 5.4: Apostasy by Adjustment-Maladjustment and Religiosity (in percentages)

	Jews		Protestants		Catholics	
Religiously Indifferent						
Adjusted	4	(298)	18	(1,189)	26	(251)
Mixed	7	(288)	20	(939)	27	(215)
Maladjusted	15	(131)	29	(360)	27	(106)
Nonreligious						
Adjusted	19	(475)	40	(1,227)	37	(216)
Mixed	28	(556)	52	(1,115)	57	(267)
Maladjusted	38	(373)	61	(637)	62	(185)

relatively weak commitment to religion largely accounts for their apostasy. By comparing the columns for the religiously indifferent with the comparable columns for the nonreligious, we find that in each religion the impact of social adjustment is strongest among the nonreligious. Similar findings were uncovered in the earlier chapters and, as the reader now knows, this indicates that we have uncovered a condition under which a given relationship is most likely to occur. In the present instance, the full force of social adjustment-maladjustment on apostasy is to be found among the nonreligious. To be both nonreligious and maladjusted is, as shown in the last row of the table, to be particularly prone to apostasy.

When commitment to higher values is considered simultaneously with religiosity, we find results very similar to those in Table 5.4, only this time the religiously indifferent Catholics behave like the others: As their commitment to higher values increases so does their apostasy rate.

Radicalism has been shown to be the trait most strongly related to nonreligiosity. How this variable interacts with religiosity to affect apostasy can be seen in Table 5.5.

Table 5.5 follows the pattern that we have seen a number of times before. Rather than one determinant of apostasy explaining the impact of another, both have an independent effect and interact so as to reinforce the effect of the other. Thus, both loss of faith and radicalism independently contribute to apostasy and each enhances the other's effect. When both are

Table 5.5: Apostasy by Radicalism and Religiosity (in percentages)

	Jews		Protestants		Catholics	
Religiously Indifferent						
Low radicalism	4	(383)	14	(1,568)	24	(307)
Medium radicalism	10	(237)	29	(780)	26	(206)
High radicalism	13	(83)	48	(94)	48	(44)
Nonreligious						
Low radicalism	17	(499)	36	(1,184)	43	(208)
Medium radicalism	28	(596)	55	(1,464)	53	(360)
High radicalism	44	(294)	77	(294)	74	(84)

present, apostasy soars, especially among the Protestants and Catholics. Thus, approximately three out of every four Protestants and Catholics who are both nonreligious and radical, apostatize. Among the comparable group of Jews, the apostasy rate is much lower, only 44 percent, but this still represents the highest rate among Jews with varying combinations of these traits. Upon close examination of the table, it will be seen that religiosity is more important than radicalism as a determinant of apostasy, but it is equally clear that religiosity does not explain the effect of radicalism. Radicalism, like maladjustment and higher values, must undermine the communal component of religious identification independent of its effects on the religious component.

The final relationship to be considered deals with the joint effect of religiosity and intellectualism on apostasy. As can be seen from Table 5.6, both have an independent effect on the apostasy rate.

Table 5.6: Apostasy by Intellectualism and Religiosity (in percentages)

	Jews		Protestants		Catholics	
Religiously Indifferent						
Low intellectualism	4	(339)	16	(1,328)	21	(318)
Medium intellectualism	9	(222)	23	(720)	33	(159)
High intellectualism	13	(125)	31	(351)	39	(72)
Nonreligious						
Low intellectualism	19	(583)	40	(1,351)	41	(305)
Medium intellectualism	29	(413)	50	(894)	55	(207)
High intellectualism	41	(359)	70	(616)	68	(123)

Table 5.6 shows that apostasy steadily increases as intellectuality and loss of religious faith increase. When one of these traits is held constant, the other continues to have an impact on apostasy. Just as when radicalism was combined with nonreligiosity, so now the combination of intellectualism and nonreligiosity is sufficient to make a majority of Protestants and Catholics apostatize.

The task of this chapter has been to assess the role of religiosity in apostasy and religious identification. At stake has been the dual-component theory of religious identification advanced by Lenski and Herberg and others, namely, that such an identity is composed of both a religious commitment and a commitment to the social group comprised of those with the same religious identity. Were loss of religious faith the sole determinant of apostasy, the apostasy-related traits should have their effect because they undermine religious commitment. These traits were found to be related to nonreligiosity, but in every instance the original relationships held among the religiously indifferent and those who viewed themselves as nonreligious. (The germs of apostasy had relatively little impact among the religious in each religion, supporting the notion that religiosity is a sufficient condition for identification.) Although loss of religiosity was a powerful determinant of apostasy, especially among the Protestants and Catholics, it did not explain the impact of the other determinants of apostasy, such as maladjustment, commitment to higher values, radicalism and intellectualism. These factors played a critical role in determining whether the less religiously committed in each religion retained their religious identity or became apostates. These results can only mean that identification with a religious community is based on more than religiosity. The various determinants of apostasy not only erode religious commitment but they undermine the particularistic commitment to the religious group as well. In short, loss of religion is at best a necessary condition for apostasy. Whether apostasy follows upon the loss of faith depends in large part on whether the other factors that undermine commitment to the religious community are present.

Chapter 6

THE COLLEGE AND APOSTASY

One of the important questions in an analysis of apostasy among college graduates is the extent to which the college experience itself plays a role in generating apostasy. Many studies have been made of the impact of college on values and attitudes of students and the results have been rather mixed. The classic study of this type is the famous Bennington study by Theodore Necomb.[1] This research demonstrated dramatic changes in the values of upper-middle-class girls as a result of their experience at a high-quality progressive school. But other studies have failed to find momentous changes. Jacobs, in his review of much of this research, concludes that the college experience has relatively little impact on students' value-orientations.[2] Parker's review of the literature dealing specifically with the impact of college on religious belief concludes that the college experience tends to liberalize religious belief, although many of these changes were presumably set off before the student entered college.

> The evidence would suggest that most students begin to experience a religious change much earlier than college, beginning at the age of fifteen. College serves to allow some to make pronounced changes, many to question and explore on an intellectual level, and most to clarify and integrate.[3]

The hypothesis that the college experience itself is crucial to apostasy thus finds little unequivocal support from the literature. Nonetheless, such an hypothesis is highly plausible. In most colleges, students are exposed to ideas which seriously question fundamentalistic religious beliefs (the literature does show that religious beliefs tend to shift from fundamentalistic to liberal during college). Furthermore, for most students college represents a departure from the family and incorporation into a peer culture. Familial influences which, we have seen, play an important role in sustaining a religious identification, are likely to decline when the student is away at college. The college peer group is typically a breeding ground for new ideas, new styles of thought and behavior.

To answer definitively the question of whether apostasy develops in college, we would need to know whether students identified with a religion at the time they entered college. The NORC study does not have such data, for it began only when these students were completing their senior year. But on the fourth wave, administered when the graduates were out of college for three years, they were asked to report what their religion was when they started college. This kind of question is open to the criticism that the graduate's recollection of his feelings at that earlier time is influenced by subsequent events. Even if all the apostates report that they did have a religious identity at the start of college, they might be accused of rewriting history. In spite of its shortcomings, this retrospective question will be considered for what clues it might provide to the role of the college. We also know whether the students lived at home or away from home while attending college. If the shift from the family to the peer group is relevant to apostasy, we should find higher apostasy rates among those who lived away from home. Most importantly, we know the college that the student attended and close analysis of the distribution of apostasy in different types of colleges will provide important clues to the role of the college in either generating apostasy or sustaining religious identification.

The retrospective question on religion at the start of college would suggest that college is indeed a breeding ground for apostasy. In each religion, substantially fewer were apostates at the beginning of college than at the end of the senior year. For Jews, the initial apostasy rate was 4 percent, compared with 13 percent when these students were seniors; for Protestants, the figures were 5 percent and 12 percent; and for Catholics, 2 percent and 7 percent. Among Jews and Catholics, the rate would appear to have more than tripled during the college years and among Protestants, to have more than doubled.

Living with parents during the college years rather than on campus tends to sustain a religious identity in each religion. The Jewish apostasy rate among those who lived at home was 10 percent, compared with 15 percent for those who lived away from home; for Protestants, the difference was in the same direction, although the gap was smaller, as 11 percent of those who lived at home became apostates, as did 13 percent of those who lived away from home; for Catholics, the apostasy rate for those living at home was 5 percent, compared with 9 percent for those living away from home. These findings are in keeping with the idea that greater involvement in college life is conducive to apostasy.

College Characteristics and Apostasy

The 34,000 college seniors who responded to the 1961 questionnaire were sampled from some 135 colleges, which in turn were sampled from the universe of four-year American colleges and universities. These 135 schools represent the full spectrum of institutions of higher learning, from teachers' colleges to engineering schools, from small liberal arts colleges to large state universities, from elite private universities to Protestant and Catholic denominational schools. Given the wide variation in types of schools, it should come as no surprise that apostasy varies greatly from school to school. Among the 135 colleges, there were 38 that had apostasy rates under 5 percent, including some 14 schools that had no apostates at all. At the other extreme were 13 colleges that had overall apostasy rates of 20 percent or more, the highest rate at any school being 30 percent. To analyze the variation in college rates of apostasy, we shall classify schools in two ways, first, according to an objective measure of their quality and second, according to commonly understood types, such as Ivy League schools, engineering schools, Catholic colleges, Protestant colleges, public universities, Southern colleges, and so forth.

SCHOOL QUALITY AND APOSTASY

Measuring school quality in some objective fashion is at best a difficult task, and no classification scheme has yet emerged that does not do injustice to a number of colleges. This problem has confronted several other research projects. A tentative solution was found in the study of college teachers during the McCarthy era reported in *The Academic Mind.*[4] In that study, a measure of quality was developed based on five characteristics of colleges typically reported in reference books. These characteristics refer mainly to the facilities of the college, such as the size of its library, the ratio of library books to students, the proportion of Ph.D.'s on the faculty, the student-faculty ratio, and the economic resources of the college reflected in its endowment and tuition fees. This index of quality does full justice to the schools that are widely recognized as superior, such as Harvard, Yale, Columbia, and the University of California. Moreover, it sorts out well those that the general consensus would label decidedly inferior. But because the index relies so heavily on resources and ratios of resources to students, it does less than full justice to the large city universities that many would acknowledge are good schools. For example, the City College of New York, which has a rather good reputation and has produced more than its share of scholars, does not fare too well on an index of this sort. Nonetheless, in spite of its shortcomings, this index has proven its worth in *The Academic Mind* and in other studies since then, and we have adopted it to classify our 135 colleges according to their quality. The relationship between school quality and apostasy can be seen from Table 6.1.

Table 6.1: Apostasy According to School Quality for Each Religion (in percentages)

School Quality	Jewish Rate	Protestant Rate	Catholic Rate	All Religions
Low	10 (30)	5 (1,689)	5 (368)	5 (2,087)
Medium low	11 (1,428)	9 (3,548)	5 (2,691)	8 (7,422)
Medium high	11 (940)	11 (7,880)	7 (3,050)	10 (12,043)
High	18 (1,129)	19 (5,016)	10 (1,841)	17 (7,986)

The last column of Table 6.1 shows the apostasy rate for each quality level irrespective of religion. By reading down the column, it can be readily seen that apostasy increases as school quality increases. Furthermore, this overall trend is reflected in each religion to differing degrees. The Protestant students are most responsive to school quality in that their apostasy rate rises most sharply. The Jewish students show a similar pattern as do, to a somewhat lesser degree, the Catholics. In fact, the Catholic apostasy rate in the highest-quality schools is double that in the lowest-quality schools. Whether this finding means that apostates are attracted to the better-quality colleges or whether such schools contribute to apostasy is not clear from this table. Most likely both processes are at work. We have already established that the more intellectual students are more likely to apostatize, and the high-quality schools are, of course, likely to recruit the more intellectual students. But at the same time, the high-quality schools undoubtedly provide an environment most challenging to traditional beliefs and to identities based on ascribed characteristics. Later we shall try to untangle these processes and assess the relative importance of each.

SCHOOL TYPE AND APOSTASY

American colleges and universities can be classified in many different ways apart from quality, for example, in terms of the type of curriculum offered, size, region, type of control, religious affiliation, sex of student body, and so forth. For the purposes of this study, we have developed an ad hoc classification that cuts across these different dimensions. Our objective is to identify types that are easily understood and relevant to apostasy. Thus, we have distinguished between twelve types of schools encompassing all one hundred and thirty-five colleges. Some of these types are quite obvious, for example, Catholic colleges, Protestant denominational schools, teachers colleges, and engineering schools. In addition, the sample contains seven of the eight Ivy League schools and these have been grouped together. Some fourteen of the colleges are located in big cities and are largely commuting schools. Five of these are in California and five in the New York metropolitan area. These commuting schools constitute yet another type. Schools that do not readily fall into these categories are classified largely by region and type of control. Thus, one type consists of all Southern colleges and universities, most of which are public. Still another type consists of Midwestern and Western public schools, the largest of our types. Included here are eight of the Big Ten schools and some twenty-four schools in all. The next category, although really part of the previous one, consists of four large California universities which we have kept separate because of their unusual apostasy rates. Three other kinds of schools complete the typology, privately controlled Midwestern schools, Mid-Atlantic schools not elsewhere classified, and small, high-quality liberal arts colleges.

Of the twelve types of schools that we have distinguished, four have apostasy rates considerably below average. These are the Catholic schools, teachers colleges, Southern colleges, and Protestant denominational schools. It may be noted that three of these types, the exception being Southern colleges, were referred to in *The Academic Mind* as *traditional* schools.[5] Table 6.2 compares the apostasy rates in each religion at these four types of schools.

The striking thing about Table 6.2 is the virtual absence of apostasy among the Catholics who attend Catholic colleges. The Catholic college clearly serves the function of sustaining a religious identity and, since more than 40 percent of the

Table 6.2: Apostasy by Religion at Types of Schools with Low Apostasy Rates (in percentages)

School Type	Jewish Rate		Protestant Rate		Catholic Rate		Total School Rate	
Catholic colleges	2	(43)	8	(72)	1	(3,630)	1	(3,567)
Teachers colleges	2	(43)	7	(477)	7	(712)	7	(712)
Southern colleges	10	(259)	6	(4,439)	8	(474)	6	(5,172)
Protestant colleges	17	(29)	6	(1,562)	8	(161)	6	(1,752)

Catholics attended Catholic colleges, we can now better understand the overall low rate of apostasy among Catholics. Even the relatively small number of Jews who attend Catholic colleges have no difficulty retaining their religious identity. At teachers colleges and Southern colleges it will be noted that all the religious groups have similar low rates of apostasy. The one exception to this pattern is the relatively high rate of apostasy among Jews at the Protestant colleges, but little credence can be given to this rate since there are so few Jews (only twenty-nine) in these schools. The low-apostasy schools shown in Table 6.2, to borrow the term used in *The Academic Mind,* can be characterized as traditional schools. In that study, it was shown that the traditional schools were generally of lower quality than the secular schools and we now see that such schools are more likely to sustain a religious identity among their students.

Five of the school types have what might be considered average or slightly above-average apostasy rates. These are the big-city commuter schools, Midwestern and Western public colleges, Midwestern private colleges, the Mid-Atlantic universities, and the engineering schools.[6] The apostasy rates for each religion at these schools are shown in Table 6.3.

Of the various types shown in Table 6.3, we find that the private Midwestern schools and the engineering schools have somewhat high apostasy rates, mainly because of the relatively high rates among the Protestants attending these schools. More striking are the rates of apostasy among the Catholics attending the types of schools shown here. It will be remembered that the apostasy rate for all Catholic students was only 7 percent. The Catholics attending these secular schools thus have apostasy

Table 6.3: Apostasy by Religion at Types of Schools with Medium Apostasy Rates (in percentages)

School Type	Jewish Rate	Protestant Rate	Catholic Rate	Total School Rate
Big-city commuter	12 (1,540)	12 (1,823)	10 (1,248)	11 (4,611)
Midwest-West public	14 (319)	13 (5,611)	10 (1,101)	12 (7,031)
Middle Atlantic university	10 (113)	10 (547)	11 (239)	11 (899)
Midwest private	13 (77)	17 (415)	10 (80)	15 (572)
Engineering	13 (251)	20 (673)	13 (433)	16 (1,357)

rates substantially above average. When the Catholics do not attend Catholic colleges and other traditional schools, they appear to be as susceptible to apostasy as Jews and Protestants. This conclusion is reinforced when we examine the schools with unusually high rates of apostasy, the Ivy League Colleges, the small high-quality liberal arts colleges and the major California universities. These data are shown in Table 6.4.

Table 6.4: Apostasy by Religion at Types of Schools with High Apostasy Rates (in percentages)

Type of School	Jewish Rate	Protestant Rate	Catholic Rate	Total School Rate
Ivy League colleges	15 (562)	23 (1,056)	23 (299)	20 (1,917)
Small high-quality colleges	28 (101)	22 (696)	26 (77)	23 (874)
Major California universities	23 (190)	28 (805)	25 (197)	27 (1,192)

The first thing to be noted about the types of schools with high apostasy rates is that they tend to be high-quality institutions. This is certainly true of the Ivy League schools. It is also true of the small liberal arts colleges and, to a great extent, it is true of the California schools. Apostasy, then, is most likely to be found among the students who attend the better colleges. There are a number of points of interest in Table 6.4. The Catholics, for the first time, have apostasy rates as high or higher than those in the other religions. In the Ivy

League schools, the Catholics have as high a rate as the Protestants, as almost one in every four of them apostatize. The Jews at such schools, in contrast, have a relatively low rate, only slightly higher than the overall Jewish rate. The Catholic apostasy rate is even higher at the high-quality, small liberal arts colleges and the major California schools. This is in sharp contrast to the picture at the Catholic colleges, where hardly any Catholics apostatize. The Catholic rate in these high-quality secular schools is more than three times the average Catholic rate.

The data presented in Table 6.4 (as in the previous tables) are based on the aggregate of schools within each type, and the question might be raised as to the amount of variation within each type. The four California schools show the least variation, as the apostasy rates for these schools range from 20 percent to 29 percent. Among the Ivy League schools, the range is somewhat greater, from 16 percent to 30 percent, and among the five small, high-quality liberal arts colleges the range is from 15 percent to 29 percent. Thus, all the schools of these types have apostasy rates substantially above average.

The distribution of apostasy among different types of schools has been informative. We have seen that the greater strength of the Catholic community in retaining the loyalties of its college graduates, compared with the Jewish and Protestant communities, is closely linked to the existence of Catholic institutions of higher learning. Thus, more than 40 percent of the Catholics attend such schools and almost none of them apostatize. But when Catholics go to secular schools, particularly the better ones, their apostasy rates increase greatly and are as high as or even higher than those of Protestants and Jews. Furthermore, we have learned that it is the high-quality secular institutions, in contrast with the relatively low-quality and more traditional schools (represented by Catholic colleges, Protestant colleges, teachers colleges, and Southern colleges), that harbor the students inclined toward apostasy.

The causal problem, however, still remains. Do the secular, high-quality institutions have higher apostasy rates because they attract and recruit students who have weak religious identities, or does the climate of opinion at these schools lead students to apostatize? Most likely, both processes are at work. Certainly the climate at a religiously controlled school must reinforce the religious identification that the student brings to college, whereas there is little in the climate of the high-quality, secular school that would perform this function. But whether the college experience at the high-quality, secular school is an *active* force eroding religious identification is another matter. It must be remembered that even at these schools, the greater majority have no difficulty retaining their religious identification. Thus, no school in the sample had an apostasy rate higher than 30 percent. The critical issue is to sort out the relative effects of recruitment and the college experience and assess the importance of each. The remainder of this chapter will attempt to cope with this problem.

The Role of the College in Apostasy

A number of characteristics of students have been identified as related to apostasy, characteristics that have been referred to as apostasy-provoking traits. To sort out the selection-recruitment process from the experience of college (socialization), we shall examine the impact of these traits in colleges with varying degrees of apostasy. If selective recruitment is the critical factor behind differences in college rates of apostasy, we should find that school apostasy rates are entirely due to the proportions of students with apostasy-related traits. Thus, the small liberal arts colleges, the Ivy League schools, the major California universities, and other schools with high apostasy rates should have disproportionate numbers of students with these traits and, when the traits are taken into account, the school differences in apostasy should disappear. The selective-recruitment hypothesis would predict that the intellectually oriented, the maladjusted, the nonreligious, the radicals, and those committed to higher values will have the same probability of becoming apostates regardless of the type of school they attend. But if the school experience is relevant and contributes to apostasy, we should find that school differences persist even when these traits are held constant. Regardless of whether students possess apostasy-provoking traits, those attending certain schools should be more prone to apostasy than those attending other schools. The method of testing the conflicting hypotheses of selection and socialization thus rests upon examining both type of school and apostasy-related traits simultaneously.

A technical question now arises. How should schools be classified for the purposes of this test? There are two possibilities. We could deal with the ad hoc typology of schools, separating schools into those with low-, medium- and high-apostasy scores. But this is only an approximation of what we want, which is to separate schools, rather than types, according to their apostasy scores. As already noted, within each type of school, there is some variation in school rates; for example, one Ivy League school has only a moderate rate, although most Ivy League schools have relatively high rates. A more appropriate method of classifying schools for the purposes of this analysis is to use the school apostasy rate. These rates have been calculated for the school as a whole ignoring religion of origin of the respondents. Three distinctions have been made in this variable. Schools with a "low" apostasy rate are those with rates of under 7 percent. The "medium" category consists of schools with rates between 7 and 16 percent and the "high" category of schools with rates of 17 percent and over. Of the 135 schools in the sample, 54 are thus classified as low on apostasy, 55 as medium, and 26 as high. Although many more schools appear in the low category than in the high, the latter are mainly large schools with the result that a substantial number of seniors are from high-apostasy schools.

The recruitment hypothesis holds that schools differ in apostasy because of different proportions of students with apostasy-provoking traits. Whether this is true or not can be seen from Table 6.5.

By reading across the rows of Table 6.5 we see that apostasy-related characteristics become more frequent as college apostasy increases. The trend is most pronounced for intellectuality and nonreligiosity. The chief respect in which the low-

Table 6.5: Apostasy-Related Traits by School Apostasy Rate (in percentages)

	School Apostasy Rate		
Apostasy Trait	Low	Medium	High
Higher values (high)	12	13	20
Maladjusted	9	11	14
Radicalism (high)	4	6	8
Intellectuality (high)	10	13	20
Nonreligious	7	18	32

and high-apostasy schools differ is in the proportion of nonreligious students they have, the factor most strongly related to apostasy. But the religious variable, perhaps more than the others, is apt to be affected by the college climate. From Parker's review of the literature we know that certain types of schools contribute to a shift from fundamentalistic to liberal religious views or what Goldsen et al. call "secular religion." To a somewhat lesser extent, the college context might also have an influence on the other apostasy-provoking traits. Some students are apt to develop an intellectual orientation or a radical perspective as a result of their college experience. To the extent that the college is a significant factor in the development of these traits, the task of unraveling the time order becomes much more difficult. The contamination that might result from the college stimulating the apostasy-related trait can only work against the hypothesis that the college differences will persist when the traits of apostasy are held constant. Should such college differences be found, we are on even safer ground in inferring that the college context contributes to apostasy.

Having seen that students at low- and high-apostasy schools differ with regard to the apostasy-provoking traits, a finding in keeping with the selective-recruitment hypothesis, we must now consider whether this explains the school differences in apostasy. This in turn requires examining the simultaneous impact of each of these traits and college apostasy on individual apostasy. We begin by presenting in Table 6.6 the joint effect of maladjustment and school apostasy on individual apostasy.

Table 6.6: The Joint Effect of Adjustment-Maladjustment and College Apostasy Rate on Individual Apostasy in Each Religious Group (in percentages)

Religion of Origin	Adjusted-Maladjusted: Adjusted	Mixed	Maladjusted
Jews			
Low-apostasy schools	3 (146)	4 (93)	15 (40)
Medium-apostasy schools	6 (918)	11 (748)	23 (297)
High-apostasy schools	10 (548)	20 (507)	34 (251)
Protestants			
Low-apostasy schools	3 (3,399)	6 (1,504)	17 (363)
Medium-apostasy schools	8 (5,397)	25 (2,830)	27 (837)
High-apostasy schools	17 (2,083)	28 (1,299)	43 (463)
Catholics			
Low-apostasy schools	1 (2,498)	2 (1,474)	5 (469)
Medium-apostasy schools	8 (1,932)	15 (817)	25 (285)
High-apostasy schools	12 (498)	24 (360)	36 (120)

The rows of Table 6.6 report what we already know, namely as maladjustment increases, so does apostasy. Of much more relevance are the patterns shown in the columns of the table. Even when position on adjustment-maladjustment is held constant, individual apostasy in each religion increases as the school rate of apostasy increases. At first glance this might seem to be tautological. Of course one would expect more people to be apostates at schools with high apostasy rates. But this finding could have been the result of the greater pool of students who are maladjusted at the high-apostasy schools. If that were the case, the column figures would not reveal a trend. But, in fact, the adjusted and mixed, as well as maladjusted, experience more apostasy as the school apostasy rate increases. Thus, the column trends are by no means tautological. They clearly indicate that the school context does have an impact on apostasy independent of the predisposing trait. Even those who do not have the predisposing trait are more likely to apostatize at such schools.

When commitment to higher values is considered simultaneously with the school apostasy rate, we find results similar to Table 6.6. Whether students score low, medium or high on higher values, they are more likely to apostatize as the school apostasy rate increases. For example, Catholics who score low on higher values have only a 1 percent rate of apostasy at low-apostasy schools, but at high-apostasy schools this rate increases to 16 percent, and the pattern is even more pronounced among Catholics who score medium and high on higher values. Again, the school differences in apostasy cannot be explained by their differential recruitment of students with an apostasy-provoking trait.

Whether differential recruitment of radical students explains college differences in apostasy can be seen from Table 6.7.

Table 6.7: The Joint Effect of Radicalism and College Apostasy on Individual Apostasy (in percentages)

	Radicalism		
Religion of Origin	Low	Medium	High
Jews			
Low-apostasy schools	2 (171)	7 (76)	19 (32)
Medium-apostasy schools	5 (1,052)	14 (675)	28 (236)
High-apostasy schools	10 (615)	22 (474)	34 (217)
Protestants			
Low-apostasy schools	2 (3,803)	9 (1,332)	31 (131)
Medium-apostasy schools	6 (6,192)	21 (25,491)	42 (323)
High-apostasy schools	14 (615)	37 (1,281)	59 (196)
Catholics			
Low-apostasy schools	1 (2,963)	3 (1,292)	7 (186)
Medium-apostasy schools	7 (1,603)	18 (788)	34 (143)
High-apostasy schools	12 (555)	27 (350)	45 (73)

The patterns of Table 6.7 are in keeping with the findings for maladjustment and higher values. Although radicalism has a powerful effect on apostasy when college apostasy is held constant (the rows of the table), the college context has a strong effect when radicalism is held constant (the columns). These patterns hold in each religion and are particularly strong among the Protestants and Catholics. Just as maladjustment and higher values failed to explain why some colleges have higher apostasy rates than others, so radicalism fails to explain the college differences, and individual students are very much affected by these college differences.

When the impact of intellectuality on individual apostasy is examined in the context of college apostasy, results similar to those in Tables 6.6 and 6.7 are found. As the college apostasy rate increases, so does individual apostasy, whether the students score low, medium, or high on intellectuality. For example, among those least inclined to apostasy, those who score low on intellectuality, the Jewish apostasy rate increases from 1 percent to 12 percent as the college apostasy rate increases from low to high; among Protestants, the low-intellectual students show an increase in apostasy from 3 percent to 18 percent; and for Catholics in this low group, apostasy climbs from 1 percent to 14 percent as the school apostasy rate increases. Similar patterns are found for those who are in the medium and high groups on intellectuality. That school differences survive when intellectuality is taken into account is further support for the socialization, as opposed to recruitment, hypothesis for the connection between college and apostasy.

The fifth test of the socialization hypothesis rests upon the joint effects of college apostasy and religiosity. As noted, this individual trait, perhaps more than the others, is susceptible to a school influence. If school differences disappear when religiosity is held constant, we could not be certain that this would rule out the impact of the college context, for the college experience could have undermined the religious commitment. But if college differences persist even when religiosity is held constant, we have particularly strong grounds for attributing a causal role to the college experience. Whether this is the case can be seen from Table 6.8.

Although similar to the earlier tables, there is one important respect in which the patterns of Table 6.8 are different. Reading down the columns, we find that the religious students (the first column) are impervious to the campus environment. Even at high-apostasy schools, hardly any religious students apostatize. This is not surprising, for we have seen earlier that religiosity is a sufficient condition for continued identification with a religious group. But among those lacking a strong religious commitment, the religiously indifferent and the nonreligious, the college impact in each religious group is quite evident. This

Table 6.8: The Joint Effect of College Apostasy and Religiosity on Individual Apostasy (in percentages)

Religion of Origin	Religiosity: Religious	Indifferent	Nonreligious
Jews			
Low-apostasy schools	0 (162)	0 (51)	21 (63)
Medium-apostasy schools	1 (822)	5 (402)	25 (710)
High-apostasy schools	2 (395)	12 (264)	31 (631)
Protestants			
Low-apostasy schools	1 (4,336)	15 (445)	36 (411)
Medium-apostasy schools	2 (6,208)	18 (1,338)	47 (1,433)
High-apostasy schools	3 (1,970)	28 (705)	56 (1,135)
Catholics			
Low-apostasy schools	0 (4,021)	9 (191)	25 (117)
Medium-apostasy schools	2 (1,940)	32 (272)	58 (293)
High-apostasy schools	1 (659)	45 (109)	65 (198)

is particularly true among the Catholics. Religiously indifferent Catholics attending low-apostasy schools seldom apostatize (only 9 percent), but at high-apostasy schools such Catholics apostatize quite frequently (45 percent). Similarly, only 25 percent of the nonreligious Catholics apostatize at the low-apostasy schools, whereas fully 65 percent do at the high-apostasy schools. Thus, whether an absence of religious feeling will lead to abandoning a religious commitment depends very much on the type of college one attends.

In the five tests of the relevance of the college to apostasy presented so far the data show that college does indeed have an impact, for college differences persist even when apostasy-provoking traits are taken into account. All of the traits presented up till now could conceivably have been influenced by the college experience as well. If certain types of colleges do indeed contribute to the development of higher values, radicalism, intellectualism, and a loss of religious faith, the impact of the college on apostasy would be stronger than the results shown. In short, what we have taken as evidence of selection might also be due in part to socialization. That college differences persisted in spite of this possible contamination lends all the more significance to the validity of the socialization hypothesis.

The next test of the socialization hypothesis rules out the possibility of contamination, for it refers to experiences that clearly precede the college experience in time, the quality of parental relations during childhood. If selection is the reason why some colleges have higher rates than others, we should find that the high-apostasy schools recruit disproportionate numbers who have had poor relations with their parents. But if school differences persist even when quality of parental relations is held constant, this would support the socialization hypothesis of a college impact on apostasy. The data are presented in Table 6.9.

Table 6.9: The Joint Effect of Quality of Parental Relations and College Apostasy Rate on Individual Apostasy Within Each Religious Group (in percentages)

Religion of Origin	Quality of Parental Relations		
	Good	Fair	Poor
Jews			
Low-apostasy schools	2 (95)	8 (64)	0 (20)
Medium-apostasy schools	6 (642)	11 (379)	23 (202)
High-apostasy schools	12 (404)	24 (328)	31 (135)
Protestants			
Low-apostasy schools	4 (2,079)	7 (870)	6 (484)
Medium-apostasy schools	8 (3,701)	15 (1,799)	16 (867)
High-apostasy schools	17 (1,498)	27 (879)	33 (382)
Catholics			
Low-apostasy schools	1 (1,599)	3 (755)	2 (369)
Medium-apostasy schools	8 (863)	15 (521)	20 (264)
High-apostasy schools	14 (305)	16 (203)	33 (109)

Inspection of the rows and columns of the table show that both the individual property, quality of parental relations, and the group property, the school apostasy rate, independently affect individual apostasy. In one respect, this table is the obverse of the previous table dealing with religiosity. There we saw that a religious commitment was an antidote to the environmental effect. In this table, we observe that the individual property of parental relations has no impact on apostasy at schools that have low-apostasy rates. This is in sharp contrast with the behavior of the other apostasy germs examined in the previous tables. In short, the environmental property serves as an antidote to the individual property.

Six tests of the socialization hypothesis have been presented and in each the hypothesis has survived. But before the findings can be accepted as demonstrating a college effect on apostasy, a serious criticism must be considered. In each instance, we have examined a single trait at a time. But it is quite likely that the number of apostasy traits students have is also related to type of school or the school apostasy rate. Thus, students who possess one of these attributes at a high-apostasy school may not really be comparable to students who possess the same attribute at a low-apostasy school because they may have more of the other traits as well. This criticism can be met by holding roughly constant the number of apostasy "germs" students have. If the college context is significant for apostasy, we should find that college differences persist when the number of traits is held constant.

We have classified all the college seniors according to the number of the following attributes they possess: 1) a strong commitment to higher values, 2) maladjustment, 3) a high score on radicalism, 4) a high score on intellectualism, 5) nonreligiosity, and 6) poor parental relations. As expected, the number of these traits that students have is related to the school apostasy rate. At the low-apostasy schools, approximately two-thirds of the students have none of these traits, whereas at the high-apostasy schools, less than two-fifths are without any of these traits. Table 6.10 shows the joint effect of school apostasy and number of predisposing traits on individual apostasy. (This table is limited to the 1964 data which permitted measurement of the quality of parental relations.)

The rows of Table 6.10 tell us what we already know: whatever the college rate of apostasy, the more apostasy-provoking traits the seniors have, the more likely they are to become apostates. But the columns of Table 6.10 are of central interest. They provide the most stringent test yet of the

Table 6.10: The Joint Effect of College Apostasy and Predisposing Traits on Individual Apostasy (in percentages)

Religion of Origin	Number of Predisposing Traits: None	One	Two	Three	Four-Six
Jews					
Low-apostasy schools	0 (83)	2 (51)	0 (23)	19 (18)	0 (6)
Medium-apostasy schools	1 (382)	4 (431)	13 (228)	33 (117)	48 (65)
High-apostasy schools	3 (191)	14 (259)	21 (203)	38 (114)	47 (89)
Protestants					
Low-apostasy schools	1 (2,166)	6 (959)	20 (231)	44 (59)	62 (13)
Medium-apostasy schools	3 (3,611)	15 (1,851)	31 (624)	51 (198)	63 (83)
High-apostasy schools	6 (1,212)	24 (892)	41 (415)	63 (172)	72 (68)
Catholics					
Low-apostasy schools	0 (1,615)	1 (739)	6 (271)	11 (76)	23 (22)
Medium-apostasy schools	4 (902)	14 (487)	30 (175)	56 (54)	70 (30)
High-apostasy schools	5 (287)	20 (194)	34 (98)	50 (20)	83 (18)

socialization hypothesis. That the college environment does have an impact on apostasy is shown by the patterns in the columns for each religion. As the school rate of apostasy increases, so does the likelihood of individual apostasy when the number of predisposing traits is held roughly constant. The college effect is weakest among those who have no apostasy traits at all, although, even in this group, a slight college effect can be detected. Among those with one, two, three or more apostasy germs, the college impact is quite pronounced, especially among the Protestants and Catholics.

Table 6.10 provides further evidence of the power of the Catholic colleges to retain the loyalty of Catholics. Among Protestants and Jews, the possession of a number of the apostasy traits is likely to lead to apostasy whatever the college rate of apostasy. But among Catholics, those attending low-apostasy schools, which are primarily the Catholic colleges, are not likely to apostatize even when they have four or more of the germs of apostasy. But once the college rate of apostasy increases somewhat, these highly vulnerable Catholics are especially likely to apostatize, their rate climbing to 83 percent in the high-apostasy schools. Finally, a comparison of the three religions shows that the Jews are not as affected by the college environment as are the Protestants and Catholics in that the percentage differences in the columns are not as pronounced for the Jews. By the same token, the Catholics seem to be most influenced by the college environment as Catholic apostasy increases most sharply with school apostasy.

This chapter explored college differences in apostasy and sought to unravel the processes of selective recruitment and socialization as explanations for the observed differences in college rates of apostasy. Apostasy was found to be related to quality of school. A more detailed typology of colleges showed that the high-quality secular colleges have the highest apostasy rates, while the more traditional schools, those that are religiously controlled, teachers colleges and Southern colleges, have the lowest apostasy rates. In between, with moderate rates of apostasy, are a great variety of public and private colleges located in the Mid-Atlantic, Midwestern, and Western states, perhaps the most striking discovery related to the low apostasy rate among the Catholic graduates. We have seen that more than two out of every five Catholics attended a Catholic college and that these Catholics hardly ever apostatize, regardless of whether they have apostasy-provoking traits. The Catholic college thus emerges as a strong antidote to apostasy. Quite strikingly, when Catholics attend secular colleges, particularly those of high quality, they are just as prone to apostasy as the Jews and Protestants, if not more so.

The critical analytical task of the chapter has been to sort out the processes of selection and socialization to see whether the college experience in any way contributes to apostasy. By holding constant the predisposing traits we were able to show that the college context does affect apostasy independent of the recruitment process. The more specific mechanisms through which the college context has its effect on apostasy remain to be explored in future research. We do not know whether the impact is due primarily to the faculty and formal courses, to the peer group, or both. But it is nonetheless clear that something happens to students who attend particular types of colleges that makes them prone to apostasy. This conclusion holds for all three religious groups, but the college impact, as we saw, is not as great on the Jews as it is on the Protestants and Catholics. This differential impact of the college environment can well be explained by differences in the bases of identification with the religious community on the part of Jews, Protestants, and Catholics. We have seen that Jewish identity is based much more on the component of communality than on religiosity, whereas the reverse is true of Catholic identity (with the Protestants in between). The college experience, particularly at the better colleges, stimulates free inquiry, encourages the questioning of dogma, and undermines the force of tradition and authority, all of which combine to shake fundamentalistic religious belief. On this basis we would expect that Catholic identification would be much more affected by the college environment than Jewish identification, an expectation borne out by the data.

NOTES

1. Theodore M. Newcomb, *Personality and Social Change: Attitude Formation in a Student Community,* New York: Holt, Rinehart and Winston, 1943; and Theodore M. Newcomb, *Persistence and Change: Bennington College and its Students after Twenty-Five Years,* New York: John Wiley, 1967. See also, Kenneth A. Feldman and Theodore M. Newcomb, *The Impact of College on Students,* San Francisco: Jossey-Bass, 1969.

2. Philip E. Jacobs, *Changing Values in College: An Exploratory Study of the Impact of College Teaching,* New York. Harper and Row, 1957.

3. Clyde A. Parker, *op. cit.*

4. Paul F. Lazarsfeld and Wagner Thielens, Jr., *The Academic Mind,* New York: Free Press, 1958.

5. Lazarsfeld and Thielens, Jr., *ibid.*

6. The reader should understand that the categories based on region are residual in the sense that commuting schools were so classified regardless of region, as were engineering schools, Ivy League schools, Catholic and Protestant schools.

Chapter 7

THE DYNAMICS OF APOSTASY

The preceding analysis has dealt with the question of why some college graduates no longer adhered to the religion in which they were raised, and, in fact, adhered to no religion. As graduating seniors, they were what we have called apostates. We have identified a number of characteristics that have shed light on the origins of apostasy, ranging from the quality of parental relations to personality traits of the students to the types of colleges they attended. But the preceding analysis has been based on data collected at a single point in time and thus suffers from the fallacy of treating what may be temporary truths as permanent truths. The tacit assumption of the preceding analysis has been that apostasy is a fixed trait and its correlates remained fixed in time. But upon closer examination, this conception of apostasy and its determinants is both shallow and fallacious. The preceding chapters dealt with apostasy as measured when students were about to graduate from college, a time when the influence of the college experience was probably at a peak. In the subsequent years, these graduates were subjected to all kinds of influences ranging from postgraduate study to various types of employment to marriage, and their basic value-orientations that we have seen are related to apostasy might also have changed. In short, religious identification or apostasy is neither fixed in childhood nor at the time of graduation from college, but rather is subject to flux throughout the life cycle.

As noted at the outset, the NORC study was a longitudinal one in which the 1961 graduates were reinterviewed yearly until three years after their graduation, in 1964. The 1964 survey included the same questions on religion and even inquired about the religion of the graduate's spouse if he or she was married by then. These panel data permit us to explore the dynamics of apostasy, the theme of this chapter. The analysis will be limited to a comparison of the earliest and latest points in time in this longitudinal survey, 1961 and 1964.

Four themes will be examined. First, we shall consider changes in religious identification between 1961 and 1964. This will involve comparing the 1961 and 1964 apostasy rates to see whether there is a trend toward or away from apostasy. We shall also examine the amount of change in religious status over this time period. How many 1961 identifiers in each religion had left the fold by 1964, and how many of the 1961 apostates had returned? This question deals with what is known in panel analysis as "turnover," i.e., shifts in position over time.[1]

The remaining sections of the chapter try to shed light on these shifts in religious status over the three-year period. The second theme will consider the role that the determinants of apostasy, examined in previous chapters, play in shifts in religious status. The third theme of the chapter is an elaboration of the second. Just as it is false to assume that apostasy is fixed at time of graduation, so it is false to assume that the various traits we have identified as "germs" of apostasy remain fixed. Some graduates undoubtedly become less religious or intellectual over time while others move in the opposite direction. To what extent do such shifts account for changes in religious status?

The fourth theme of the chapter focuses on the impact of intervening events in the lives of the graduates on changes in their religious identifications. By intervening events, we mean changes in the social statuses occupied by the graduates, e.g., their going to graduate school, professional school or work following graduation, the type of employment they are engaged in, whether they married, and if so, whether they married someone raised in the same religion as they or a different religion. These four themes constitute the major sections of this chapter.

Stability and Change in Religious Identification

Two conflicting theories can be offered to predict the amount of apostasy among college graduates three years after graduation. According to one view, relinquishing a religious identification is little more than a college-induced "fad," and when the graduate returns to the "real world," he quickly reverts to his religion of origin. The opposing view holds that the process of secularization continues throughout the life cycle and that college graduates, especially exposed to this process, will continue to apostatize following their graduation from college. What in fact happened three years later? The data indicate that either both of these forces are at work or that neither has much impact, for the apostasy rates in each religion three years later were quite similar to the rates in 1961. For Jews, apostasy declined by one percentage point, from 13 to 12 percent; Protestants showed the same rate of apostasy in 1961 and 1964, 11 percent; only for the Catholics did apostasy increase over this three year period, from 6 percent to 8 percent. (These figures are based on the weighted sample.)

To complete questionnaires year after year might be taken as a token of conformity and, since apostates tend to be nonconformists, perhaps they were less likely to respond in 1964. If so, the trend toward apostasy might be greater than is shown in Table 7.1. Oddly enough, this expectation of lower response by apostates holds for Protestants and Catholics whose apostasy rates either remained the same or increased, but not for Jews, whose apostasy rate declined slightly. Among Protestants, 66 percent of the 1961 identifiers responded in 1964, compared with 61 percent of the apostates. Among Catholics, the comparable figures are 62 and 57 percent, but among Jews, the 1964 response rates were similar for 1961 identifiers and apostates, 63 percent and 62 percent respectively. Had the initial apostates in each religion responded to the same degree as the identifiers three years later, the Protestants might have shown a trend toward apostasy and the Catholic trend would probably have been more pronounced. But in the one religious group that showed a slight decline in apostasy, the Jews, the discrepancy between the response rates in 1964 of the 1961 identifiers and apostates is so slight that the picture of a return to the fold for Jews appears to be correct. For reasons that remain to be explored, Jewish apostasy peaks at graduation, whereas the religious identifications of Catholics continue to erode after graduation from college, and, were all the 1961 apostates to have responded in 1964, the Protestants would probably show a trend similar to the Catholics.

Apart from trends in apostasy is the question of changes in the religious status of individuals. These are shown in Table 7.1 which presents the percentage in each religious group who remained constant or switched position over the three-year period.

Table 7.1: Turnover in Religious Status Between 1961 and 1964 (Based on the Weighted Sample, in percentages)

Religious Status in 1961	1964	Jews	Protestants	Catholics
Identifier	identifier	83	86	91
Identifier	apostate	4	4	3
Apostate	identifier	6	3	1
Apostate	apostate	7	7	5
		100	100	100
	N	(1,215)	(11,726)	(4,816)

The top and botton rows of Table 7.1 report the percentages in each religion who remained constant with respect to religious status between 1961 and 1964. Since many more Jews and Protestants than Catholics apostatized in 1961, it is hardly surprising that proportionately more Catholics were consistent identifiers and, for the same reasons, the consistent apostates are proportionately larger among Jews and Protestants than among Catholics (the fourth row of the table). Of much more interest are the middle rows which show change in religious identification between 1961 and 1964. Among Jews, we see that 4 percent who were initially identifiers joined the ranks of apostates by 1964, but they were more than offset by the 6 percent who were initially apostates but had returned to the fold by 1964. Among Protestants and Catholics the net change works in favor of apostasy. Thus, while 4 percent of the Protestants who were identifiers in 1961 had become apostates by 1964, only 3 percent of the Protestants shifted from apostasy back to a religious identification for a net loss of one percentage point. Among Catholics, the erosion of religious identification is even more severe. Three percent of the Catholics switched to apostasy after graduation, whereas only one percent, initially apostates, returned to the fold. This turnover table confirms what the trend data of Table 7.1 showed, namely that the religious identifications of Protestants and Catholics continued to erode over time, whereas the Jews managed to reclaim more of their own than they lost over the three-year period.

The question that will concern us in the remainder of the analysis will deal with the rather miniscule numbers in each religion who switched their religious identities between 1961 and 1964. Even though they constitute only 10 percent of the Jews, 9 percent of the Protestants, and 4 percent of the Catholics, these "switchers" are of strategic importance. A careful analysis of them should shed light on the forces leading to apostasy and identification.

The Traits of Apostasy in 1961 and Apostasy in 1964

A series of traits have been identified as "determinants" of apostasy, including quality of parental relations, psychological adjustment, "radicalism," intellectuality, and religiosity. In the context of the dynamics of apostasy, two questions regarding these attributes arise. First, to what extent are these 1961 attributes linked to apostasy three years later? Are the correlations as strong when these traits are related to apostasy at the later time as at the earlier time? Second, to what extent do these traits help us to understand the shifts that occurred in religious identification over the three year period? Were the former identifiers who shifted to apostasy those who had the "germs" of apostasy back in 1961 and, conversely, were the apostates who returned to the fold those in which the "germs" of apostasy were initially weak?

The answer to the first question is that the apostasy-provoking traits of the students in 1961 were as good predictors of apostasy in 1964 as in 1961. In every instance, the "germs" found to be related to apostasy in 1961 were related to apostasy in 1964 in each of the three religious groups. Sometimes the correlation in 1964 was stronger and sometimes weaker, but in most instances it was of comparable strength.

Given the continuing role of these traits in the production of apostasy, to what extent do they shed light on the shifts in religious identifications that took place between 1961 and 1964? Were the identifiers who shifted toward apostasy in the interim likely to be people who manifested the "germs" in 1961? And, conversely, were the apostates who returned to the fold those who were not too "infected" to begin with?

Of the six apostasy traits identified in the previous chapters, we shall focus on three for the purposes of this analysis: quality of parental relations, radicalism and intellectualism. The patterns shown for these items more or less hold for the other germs, "higher values," "maladjustment," and "religiosity," and hence there is little need to make this rather complex analysis even more complicated.

There are two ways of demonstrating the impact of an apostasy trait on the dynamics of apostasy: showing the amount of turnover for each value of the trait (what is known as qualified turnover) and showing the role of the trait in generating apostasy among original identifiers and preserving apostasy among original apostates. Qualified turnover is the more complicated form of analysis and thus we shall present only one table of this kind, Table 7.2, which shows the turnover in religious status for each level of parental relations.[2]

Table 7.2: Turnover in Religious Status as Qualified by Quality of Parental Relations in Each Religion of Origin (in percentages)

Religious Status 1961	1964	Quality of Parental Relations Poor	Fair	Good
Jews				
Identifier	identifier	65	81	90
Apostate	identifier	9	7	4
Identifier	apostate	7	6	3
Apostate	apostate	20	6	3
		101	100	100
	N	(337)	(664)	(1,044)
Protestants				
Identifier	identifier	68	80	88
Apostate	identifier	6	4	3
Identifier	apostate	7	6	4
Apostate	apostate	19	10	5
		100	100	100
	N	(968)	(3,023)	(6,604)
Catholic				
Identifier	identifier	76	89	94
Apostate	identifier	2	1	1
Identifier	apostate	7	4	2
Apostate	apostate	14	5	3
		99	99	100
	N	(494)	(1,231)	(2,605)

The top row in each part of Table 7.2 shows the percentage of consistent identifiers on each level of parental relations. Regardless of religion, we see that consistent identifiers increase as parental relations improve and, conversely, consistent apostates steadily increase in each religion as parental relations worsen (the fourth row in each part of the table). This is, of course, to be expected, since quality of parental relations is a significant determinant of apostasy. Of more interest are the two middle rows in each part of the table, for they report the amount of turnover in identity between 1961 and 1964. By adding the figures in the turnover cells, we make an interesting discovery. In each religion, those possessing the apostasy germ to the greatest degree, that is, those reporting poor parental relations, show the greatest instability. Among Jews, 16 percent of those in the "poor" group switched, compared with 13 percent in the "fair" group and 7 percent in the "good" group. Among Protestants, the comparable figures are 13, 10, and 7 percent, and among Catholics, 9, 5, and 3 percent. In short, those who had good relations with their parents were least likely to apostatize in the first place and they were most likely to be consistent identifiers in subsequent years.

Remaining to be considered is the direction of the change. Here the religious groups part company for the patterns are sharply different. By comparing the second and third rows, we see that among Jews, regardless of the quality of parental relations, more graduates returned to the fold than left it over the three-year period. For example, among those reporting "poor" parental relations, 9 percent shifted from apostasy to identification, whereas 7 percent changed from identification to apostasy. The same pattern appears among those reporting "fair" and "good" parental relations. Among Protestants, the reverse is found. Regardless of quality of parental relations, slightly more left the fold over the three-year period than returned, the numbers in the third row being larger than those in the second. Only among Catholics does the predisposing trait seem to affect the direction of change in the anticipated manner. Thus, among Catholics reporting "good" parental relations, hardly any change occurred, and there was little difference in the number of respondents shifting in one or the other direction. Among Catholics who had "fair" relations with their parents, there was a predominance of shifts toward apostasy rather than identification (4 percent moving from identification to apostasy, but only one percent from apostasy to identification), and among those who experienced "poor" parental relations, the trend was even more pronounced (7 percent shifting from identification to apostasy, and only 2 percent moving in the other direction).

The patterns for the Jews and Protestants shown in Table 7.2 seem to suggest that quality of parental relations had little to do with turnover in religious identification. But this is misleading, for position on this trait had a good deal to do with stability among original identifiers and apostates in each religion (the first and fourth rows). This becomes more evident when the data of Table 7.2 are presented in a different fashion, taking into account the graduate's position in 1961 as an identifier or an apostate. Table 7.3 shows the proportion of original identifiers in each religion who shifted to apostasy by 1964 according to the quality of their relationship with their parents. It also shows the proportion of original apostates who remained apostates at the later point. The percentages in this table thus refer to apostasy in 1964 for both the original identifiers and the original apostates. For the identifiers, the figures show the percentage who changed, and for the apostates the percentage who did *not* change, that is, remained apostates.

Table 7.3: Proportion of 1961 Identifiers and Apostates Who Became Apostates or Remained Apostates in 1964 by Quality of Parental Relations (in percentages)

Parental Relations	1961 Identifiers Who Became Apostates in 1964	1961 Apostates Who Remained Apostates in 1964
Jews		
Poor	10 (242)	70 (95)
Fair	7 (572)	47 (92)
Good	3 (973)	41 (71)
Protestants		
Poor	9 (719)	75 (249)
Fair	7 (2,612)	70 (411)
Good	4 (6,076)	61 (528)
Catholics		
Poor	9 (411)	86 (83)
Fair	4 (1,150)	79 (81)
Good	2 (2,504)	75 (101)

By reading down the columns, we learn that quality of parental relations does have an effect in generating apostasy among original identifiers in each religion and in preserving apostasy among the original apostates. Identifiers who reported poor parental relations were more likely to have become apostates by 1964 than identifiers who had good relations with their parents, although even in the former group the apostasy rates were low, not exceeding 10 percent. The original apostates, whatever their religion and whatever the quality of their parental relations, were more unstable. Among Jewish apostates, only those who experienced poor parental relations were likely to remain apostates. Among Jewish apostates who had fair and good parental relations, a majority had switched back to identifying with Jews by 1964. The Jewish apostates show by far the most instability, whereas the Catholic apostates show the most stability, with the Protestants in between. But even among the Catholics, quality of parental relations affected the stability of apostasy. Whereas 86 percent of the Catholic apostates who had poor relations with parents remained apostates three years later, the figure declined to 75 percent among those who had good parental relations.

Much the same results appear when we consider the influence of another germ on the dynamics of apostasy—radicalism. Turnover qualified by radicalism yields patterns similar to those in Table 7.2. The percentage of consistent identifiers steadily increases as radicalism declines, and, conversely, the percentage of consistent apostates increases as radicalism increases. The turnover patterns are also similar to those in Table 7.2. On each level of radicalism, slightly more Jews return to the fold than leave it; for Protestants the patterns are mixed, and among Catholics somewhat more leave the fold than return to it on each level of radicalism. Table 7.4 shows the role of radicalism in generating and preserving apostasy.

Reading down the first column of Table 7.4, we see that original identifiers in each religion are somewhat more likely to become apostates as they become more radical, and the second column shows that original apostates are more likely to remain apostates as they possess more of this apostasy-provoking trait. The Jewish apostates turn out to be much more unstable than the Protestant and Catholic apostates over this period, with proportionately more Jewish apostates returning to the fold whatever their level of radicalism.

Table 7.4: Proportion of 1961 Identifiers and Apostates Who Became Apostates or Remained Apostates in 1964 by Radicalism (in percentages)

Radicalism	1961 Identifiers Who Became Apostates in 1964	1961 Apostates Who Remained Apostates in 1964
Jews		
Low	3 (1,042)	40 (67)
Medium	6 (640)	52 (127)
High	10 (212)	62 (90)
Protestants		
Low	4 (7,320)	59 (461)
Medium	9 (2,609)	69 (674)
High	13 (234)	76 (177)
Catholics		
Low	3 (2,906)	70 (1,040)
Medium	5 (1,303)	83 (151)
High	8 (193)	87 (54)

When intellectualism is related to religious status at time 1 and time 2, the turnover patterns are similar to those found for the other germs. The percentage of consistent identifiers steadily increases as intellectualism declines, and consistent apostasy increases as intellectualism increases. On each level of intellectualism, slightly more Jews give up their apostasy than become new apostates, whereas for both Protestants and Catholics the percentage leaving the fold exceeds the percentage returning. Table 7.5 shows the role of intellectualism in generating apostasy among original identifiers and preserving apostasy among the original apostates.

Again, we see that a predisposing trait played a role in generating apostasy among initial identifiers and preserving apostasy among original apostates. In each religion identifiers who were committed to intellectualism showed some tendency toward apostasy, whereas those lacking this commitment experienced hardly any apostasy. And among apostates, intellectualism inhibited the tendency to return to the fold. As with the other two predisposing traits examined, we again find apostasy to be least stable among the Jews and most stable among the Catholics. Even among Jews highly committed to intellectualism, a substantial minority of the original apostates

Table 7.5: Proportion of 1961 Identifiers and Apostates Who Became Apostates or Remained Apostates by Intellectuality (in percentages)

Intellectuality	1961 Identifiers Who Became Apostates in 1964	1961 Apostates Who Remained Apostates in 1964
Jews		
High	11 (307)	61 (107)
Medium	4 (586)	47 (94)
Low	4 (1,001)	47 (77)
Protestants		
High	12 (1,018)	73 (368)
Medium	6 (2,758)	68 (400)
Low	4 (6,439)	60 (526)
Catholics		
High	8 (424)	83 (82)
Medium	4 (6,439)	86 (99)
Low	3 (2,853)	73 (122)

returned to the fold three years later, and among Jewish apostates who scored medium and low on intellectualism, more than half became identifiers in the interim. The instability of Jewish apostates in contrast with the Catholics is a reminder of the different bases of identification in these religious groups. As we have seen, Catholic identity rests largely on religiosity, whereas Jewish identity is based as much on communality as on religiosity. Once a Catholic loses faith, he is apt to leave the group for good for it is not likely that he will subsequently have the religious spark rekindled. But Jews who leave the religious group for one reason, e.g., loss of faith, can always return for another, e.g., a sense of communality with other Jews. These different meanings of religious identification no doubt account for the observed differences in the stability of apostasy between Jews and Catholics.

The Dynamics of Apostasy in Light of the Dynamics of the Apostasy Traits

In the preceding section, we examined the dynamics of apostasy in terms of the strength of the apostasy germs as measured at the time of graduation. The assumption was that over time the respondents would bring their religious identifications into harmony with their attitudes as measured when they were college seniors. But this analysis was based on a questionable premise, namely that the predisposing traits (the apostasy germs) remained fixed through the time interval. But, of course, attitudes and values, like religious identifications, change. Since predispositional traits and religious identification are both subject to change over time, the critical question becomes how shifts in religious identification can be explained by changes in the predispositional traits.

Since this analysis of mutual effects is more complicated than the analysis of "qualified turnover" in the previous section, we shall consider only two of the apostasy traits for which measurements are available at both points in time, intellectualism and the trait that, as we saw in Chapter 5, is most strongly related to apostasy, religiosity. The items used to determine career intellectuality also appeared on the fourth wave of the NORC panel study, but the measure of religiosity changed somewhat. Instead of assessing their religiosity in some absolute sense, the respondents on the fourth wave were asked to judge themselves compared with their peers. They could reply that compared with their peers they were very religious, somewhat religious, a bit religious, or not at all religious. This measure gives the appearance of a decline in religiosity over the three year period but it is likely that this decline is more a reflection of the measuring instrument than a true loss of religiosity.

One other methodological note is in order. Since the predisposing traits that we have been studying each have three categories, an examination of them for both 1961 and 1964 simultaneously with apostasy-identification for both years generates thirty-six cell tables for each religious group. Tables of such complexity are extremely hard to read and understand, and to simplify matters we shall reduce all the cells that signify change in the predisposing trait to two groups: those reflecting an increase in the trait, and those reflecting a decrease in the trait. In short, those who move from low to medium, low to high, and medium to high are grouped together in the "increase" category and, conversely, those who moved from high to medium, high to low, or medium to low comprise the "decrease" category.

To simplify the analysis still further, we shall present data bearing only on the generating and preserving effects of changes in the apostasy germ over time. Table 7.6 shows how consistency and change in commitment to intellectuality affected apostasy in 1964.

Table 7.6: Proportion of 1961 Identifiers and Apostates Who Became Apostates or Remained Apostates in 1964 by 1961-1964 Turnover in Intellectualism (in percentages)

	1961 Identifiers Who Became Apostates in 1964	1961 Apostates Who Remained Apostates in 1964
Jews		
Intellectuality increased	7 (370)	53 (64)
Intellectuality decreased	2 (357)	49 (55)
Intellectuality remained low	3 (697)	47 (34)
Intellectuality remained medium	5 (239)	40 (38)
Intellectuality remained high	15 (183)	63 (78)
Protestants		
Intellectuality increased	7 (2,149)	71 (311)
Intellectuality decreased	5 (1,476)	64 (222)
Intellectuality remained low	3 (4,594)	56 (310)
Intellectuality remained medium	6 (1,175)	64 (173)
Intellectuality remained high	14 (627)	77 (248)
Catholics		
Intellectuality increased	5 (920)	82 (68)
Intellectuality decreased	3 (603)	84 (61)
Intellectuality remained low	2 (2,063)	71 (72)
Intellectuality remained medium	4 (474)	85 (40)
Intellectuality remained high	9 (267)	83 (54)

The impact of change in intellectual commitment can be assessed by comparing the first and second rows in each part of the table. In all three religious groups, identifiers who experienced an increase in intellectual commitment were more likely to have apostatized by 1964 than identifiers whose intellectual commitment had lessened over the years. Among Jews and Protestants, an increasing intellectual commitment also had an impact on preserving apostasy. But among Catholics the tendency to remain an apostate was quite strong, and those whose intellectual commitment diminished were, if anything, slightly more likely to remain apostates than were the respondents whose intellectual commitment had grown in the interim. Of more significance, perhaps, are the patterns shown by those whose intellectual commitment remained constant over the three-year period. The data in the third, fourth, and fifth rows in each part of the table show a strain toward consistency between intellectual commitment and apostasy. Thus, in each religious group, the identifiers who were consistently nonintellectual hardly ever apostatized in subsequent years, and, conversely, in each religious group apostates who lacked intellectual moorings were most likely to return to the fold. At the other extreme, those consistently committed to intellectualism were most likely to abandon their religious identification if they had not already done so, and they were most likely to cling to apostasy if they had previously adopted this position. As shown in other tables the Jewish apostates were most unstable and the Catholic ones most stable. Among initial Jewish apostates who were consistently low or medium on intellectualism, a majority returned to the fold, and even among the Jewish apostates who were consistently intellectual a substantial minority regained a Jewish identification. In contrast, the Catholic apostates held fast on all levels of intellectualism, especially those who were on the medium or high level. Oddly enough, change in intellectualism over the three-year period among the original Catholic apostates had no bearing on the continuation of apostasy. Those whose intellectualism decreased were as likely to remain apostates as those whose intellectualism increased.

To broaden the spectrum of apostasy-provoking traits that might shed light on the dynamics of apostasy, we now consider the single most important determinant of apostasy, religiosity. In Chapter 5 we saw that religiosity played the role of a sufficient condition for a religious identification. Thus, in each religion hardly any deeply religious persons relinquished their religious identification. But to be less than fully religious was not a sufficient condition for apostasy. Other attributes, i.e., other germs of apostasy, had to be present to break the tie to the religious community. As noted before, the later measure of religiosity is not identical with the earlier one, but they are sufficiently similar to permit treating them as equivalent measures of the same concept. The task before us now is to see how shifts in religious commitment over the three-year period affected original identifiers and apostates. These data are shown in Table 7.7.

Table 7.7: Proportion of 1961 Identifiers and Apostates Who Became Apostates or Remained Apostates in 1964 by Turnover in Religiosity (in percentages)

	1961 Identifiers Who Became Apostates in 1964	1961 Apostates Who Remained Apostates in 1964
Jews		
Religiosity increased	2 (239)	23 (31)
Religiosity decreased	4 (635)	57 (28)
Religiosity remained high	1 (325)	0/1*
Religiosity remained medium	1 (176)	0/7*
Religiosity remained low	14 (419)	58 (199)
Protestants		
Religiosity increased	5 (776)	31 (222)
Religiosity decreased	8 (3,010)	66 (210)
Religiosity remained high	** (5,054)	21 (34)
Religiosity remained medium	5 (588)	35 (77)
Religiosity remained low	41 (385)	86 (653)
Catholics		
Religiosity increased	4 (175)	44 (48)
Religiosity decreased	11 (881)	88 (58)
Religiosity remained high	0.4 (3,117)	38 (8)
Religiosity remained medium	5 (95)	62 (21)
Religiosity remained low	44 (59)	94 (143)

*Hardly any Jews are located in these cells and none of them remained apostates three years later.

**Fewer than one-tenth of one percent of the religious Protestants apostatized.

Table 7.7 is quite striking in a number of respects. As in Table 7.6, whether the apostasy "germ" increased or decreased over the three-year period has a small effect on the religious status of the original identifiers. Thus, Jewish identifiers who became less religious were slightly more likely to apostatize in

1964 compared with those who became more religious (4 percent vs. 2 percent); among Protestants, the comparable figures are 8 and 5 percent; and among Catholics they are more substantial, 11 percent and 4 percent. But changes in religiosity have a profound impact on the original apostates in each religion. In every religion, an increase in religiosity leads a majority of the original apostates to return to the fold. This is especially true of the Jews, of whom only 23 percent of the original apostates who become more religious remain apostates, but it is also true of the Protestants (31 percent remaining apostates) and of the Catholics (44 percent). Conversely, a loss of religiosity was likely to lead the original apostates to cling to their position. But among Jews only a bare majority of the apostates who became less religious remained apostates; among Protestants, about two-thirds remained constant; and among Catholics, where apostasy is most firm, only a small fraction of apostates who became less religious defected from their original position.

Focusing now on those whose religious commitment remained constant over the three-year period, we find that these consistent positions had a pronounced effect on turnover in religious status. In each religious group, especially the Protestants and Catholics, original identifiers with a high dosage of the "germ," i.e., those who were consistently nonreligious, showed a tendency to apostatize after graduation. Among Jews, this rate was rather small, 14 percent, but among Protestants and Catholics it was over 40 percent. Among the original apostates, respondents who were consistently nonreligious were likely to remain apostates. This is particularly true of the nonreligious Catholic apostates, fully 94 percent of whom retained their position three years later. Of the Protestant apostates 86 percent of the consistently nonreligious remained apostates, but among Jews we find only a bare majority of the nonreligious remaining apostates (58 percent), which is further proof of the instability of Jewish apostasy. In fact, consistent commitment to intellectualism had a more preserving effect on Jewish apostasy than consistent nonreligiosity (see Table 7.6), a finding in keeping with all the prior evidence on the multiple bases of Jewish identity. Just as low religiosity reinforced apostasy in each religion, so strong religiosity sharply undermined apostasy. There was only one Jewish graduate who was consistently high on religion and had opted for apostasy, and by 1964 he had returned to the fold. Among Protestants 34 students claimed to be apostates in 1961 even though they were consistently high on religiosity, and the great majority of these (all but 21 percent) had given up their apostasy by 1964. Only a handful of Catholics were in this position, eight in all, and here too, a majority had returned to their religious group by 1964.

Tables 7.6 and 7.7 show that the dynamics of apostasy germs have a marked impact on apostasy. Those who were consistent in their positions on intellectualism and religiosity tended to change their religious identifications over time in order to make them more consistent with their value commitments. And those who changed their positions on intellectualism and religiosity tended to alter their religious statuses accordingly. The other apostasy germs for which data are available in both 1961 and 1964, radicalism, higher values, and adjustment-maladjustment, show similar patterns.

The Role of Intervening Events in the Dynamics of Apostasy

We have seen how changes in values and attitudes influenced the religious status of respondents over the three-year period. But, of course, value changes were not the only or even the most important changes to occur. Of even more significance were the shifts in social status that these graduates experienced after college. Some of them went on to graduate school; others went to work in a variety of settings; many of the respondents married, some of them outside their religion of origin, and many of the married had children by 1964. How did these intervening events, these changes in social status, affect stability and change in religious identification? We begin our analysis by considering the impact of postgraduate education.

POSTGRADUATE CAREER AND TURNOVER IN RELIGIOUS STATUS

In Chapter 4, we saw that those who chose careers requiring postgraduate study were more likely to apostatize than those who did not make such career choices. Did the experience of attending graduate school further undermine religious identification? Were respondents who did go to graduate school more likely to apostatize three years later than they were at time of graduation? And what about those who went to professional school or who did not continue their education beyond college? If students did not do postgraduate work, their apostasy level either remained the same three years later or declined. Jews in this group showed somewhat less apostasy in 1964, 8 percent compared with 10 percent in 1961; among Protestants and Catholics, the rates increased a single percentage point, from 9 to 10 percent for Protestants and from 6 to 7 percent for Catholics. Attending professional school was also associated with a decline in apostasy for the Jews, from 12 percent to 10 percent. Among Protestants, there was no change in the apostasy rate for those who went to professional school, and Catholics in this group showed an increase in the apostasy rate from 7 percent to 10 percent over the three-year period. Attending graduate school, as expected, had the greatest impact on apostasy in each religion. Among Jews, the trend from apostasy back to identification was arrested, as the proportion of apostates was 29 percent in both 1961 and 1964. Protestants in graduate school showed a 4 percent increase in apostasy, from 28 to 32 percent; and Catholics also showed a 4 percent increase, from 14 to 18 percent. As these figures demonstrate, those in each religion who attended graduate school had by far the highest apostasy rates.

The role of graduate school in generating apostasy among those who were identifiers in 1961 and in preserving apostasy among the original apostates is shown in Table 7.8.

Table 7.8: Proportion of 1961 Identifiers and Apostates Who Became Apostates or Remained Apostates in 1964 by Postgraduate Activity (in percentages)

Postgraduate Activity	1961 Identifiers Who Became Apostates in 1964	1961 Apostates Who Remained Apostates in 1964
Jews		
Graduate school	15 (2,010)	63 (83)
Professional school	4 (1,632)	47 (85)
Not in school	3 (760)	48 (83)
Protestants		
Graduate school	14 (645)	79 (247)
Professional school	6 (2,034)	69 (296)
Not in school	4 (5,870)	64 (554)
Catholics		
Graduate school	8 (310)	80 (51)
Professional school	4 (975)	86 (70)
Not in school	3 (2,171)	79 (142)

Apostasy among previous identifiers generated by graduate school was most pronounced for the Jews (15 percent), almost as great among the Protestants (14 percent), and least among the Catholics (8 percent). As expected, in each religion graduate school produced more apostasy than either professional school or no school at all. Graduate school was also most likely to preserve apostasy among Jews and Protestants; fewer apostates from these groups in graduate school returned to their original religion than did Jews and Protestants in the other settings. Oddly enough, among Catholics, where apostasy was most resistant to change whatever the setting, the professional school had a greater preserving effect than graduate school (86 percent compared with 80 percent).

The role of graduate school in generating and preserving apostasy is in keeping with the earlier findings showing that a commitment to intellectualism and to the typical home of the intellectual—the university—places considerable strain on religious identification. Intellectuals, we have argued, are not only committed to empirically based truths which make them suspicious of religious dogma, but also to the values of universalism and achievement rather than particularism and ascription, the values that are embodied in religious identifications.

The findings on the impact of graduate school were buttressed by data on the locus of employment. 1961 graduates who held jobs in 1964 were asked to identify the sector of the economy in which they were employed. Their detailed responses have been grouped into six categories for the purposes of this analysis, the critical category being employment at a university or college. Considering the fact that these people had been out of college only three years, one might ask what kind of university or college jobs they had. Perhaps some fit the category of ABD's–the well-known category of "All But Dissertation" and were employed as instructors at colleges; perhaps some were employed as full-time research assistants even while attending graduate school; and some may have been women employed as secretaries in colleges. All such people could justly claim that they were employed in a university or college. The other categories of employment included self-employed professional, business, government, elementary and secondary schools, and an "all other" category which covered research, welfare, hospital, and church organizations. One might quarrel with our grouping together nonuniversity research organizations, welfare organizations, public and private, and hospitals and church organizations, but this decision was as much pragmatic as conceptual. Not only do such work organizations seem to have something in common, e.g., a disinterested concern with the welfare of others, but the number of graduates employed in these categories is rather small and the results are not very different from one of these categories to another. The main purpose of this analysis is to show the impact of college and university employment on apostasy in contrast to other types of employment, and we can just as easily group all other types as well as distinguish them in broad categories. We present now in Table 7.9 the trends in apostasy of those employed in these different sectors according to religion of origin. The trend toward apostasy is most pronounced among the relatively small numbers in each religion who managed to obtain employment in the home of the intellectuals–the college/university. Among the Jews, apostasy in this group increased by 7 percentage points over the three

Table 7.9: 1961 and 1964 Apostasy Rates of Those Employed in Various Sectors of the Economy in 1964 by Religion of Origin (in percentages)

	Jews		Protestants		Catholics	
Locus of Employment	1961 Apostasy	1964 Apostasy	1961 Apostasy	1964 Apostasy	1961 Apostasy	1964 Apostasy
University/college	15	22 (41)	14	20 (392)	12	16 (117)
Government	9	10 (176)	11	13 (1,134)	7	9 (435)
Profession	6	0 (71)	12	10 (296)	7	4 (115)
Business	8	8 (552)	12	11 (2,925)	6	7 (1,472)
School teaching	11	7 (289)	6	7 (2,189)	5	7 (725)
All other	11	10 (132)	9	8 (887)	9	6 (349)

year period; among Protestants the increase in apostasy was 6 percentage points; and among Catholics 4 percentage points. Jews in all other types of employment (except government) manifested the trend away from apostasy documented in the earlier tables. Among Protestants the aggregate trend toward apostasy was manifested almost exclusively by those employed in an institution of higher learning. As was found for Jews, employment in government also increased apostasy slightly among the Protestants, but the other types of employment either failed to increase Protestant apostasy or contributed to its reduction. Among Catholics the impact of university/college employment was much the same as in the other religions in that it increased the apostasy rate among those who opted for these careers. The Catholic apostasy rate increased, but not as markedly, in other types of employment as well, with one exception: Catholics working as professionals showed a decline in apostasy.

MARITAL STATUS AND THE DYNAMICS OF APOSTASY

Marriage is, of course, a major event in a person's life and a substantial number of college graduates did get married in the three-year period following their graduation. (Some were married before they graduated.) Since most people marry co-religionists, it is reasonable to suppose marriage is a factor reinforcing religious identification and inducing initial apostates to return to the fold. But the facts of the matter are that marriage makes very little difference in the dynamics of apostasy. We know the marital status of the respondents at the time of graduation and three years after. Thus, we can locate all the graduates in one of five groups: a) those who were single at both times; b) those who moved from being single in 1961 to being engaged in 1964; c) those who went from single to married; d) those who were engaged in 1961 and married in 1964; and finally e) those who were married in both years. (Very few of the respondents were divorced in 1964 and these cases have been eliminated.)

Whatever the religion and whatever the category of students based on change in marital status, there was little difference between the 1961 and 1964 apostasy rates, indicating few if any trends. Of the fifteen comparisons that can be made (the five categories in each of the three religions), six involve percentage differences of only a single point and six of only two points. The largest percentage difference is only three points and occurs in three categories. Remaining single is apparently conducive to apostasy among Protestants and Catholics, but not Jews. Thus, among Protestants the apostasy rate among the singles increased (from 15 percent to 18 percent); among Catholics the singles' rate also went up (from 6 to 9 percent). But among Jews apostasy in this group declined (from 16 to 14 percent). In fact, the only group of Jews showing a slight increase in apostasy is the former singles who were engaged in 1964 (their apostasy increased from 13 percent to 15 percent). Although Catholic singles and Catholics who moved from single to engaged each showed a gain of three percentage points in apostasy (the third group with a gain this large, as noted, is the Protestant singles), neither of these groups of Catholics had the highest apostasy rates in 1961 or 1964. That honor belongs to the Catholics who were married in both years, as 11 percent of them were apostates in 1961 and 12 percent in 1964. This is probably explained by the unusually high rate of intermarriage among Catholic college graduates, a factor considered below. Thus, the mere fact of getting married or having one's marital status change from single to engaged or, for that matter, avoiding marriage has little to do with the dynamics of apostasy.

More significant than the act of marriage from the standpoint of apostasy is the fruit of marriage, whether the marriage has produced offspring or not. Having and raising children in America often involves the question of the religious identification not of the parents but of the child. Parents must make the conscious decision whether they want their child to have a religious identity, and they may decide in the affirmative in part because their children are made conscious of religion by forces outside the home, their friends and school activities. This, in turn, creates pressures on the parents to maintain a religious identity as well. The data on hand suggest that having children does contribute to the maintenance of a religious identification, and, if not to the abandonment of apostasy, at least to its retardation. This can be seen from Table 7.10.

Table 7.10: 1961 and 1964 Apostasy Rates of Those Respondents Who Were Married in 1964 According to Whether They Had Children (in percentages)

	Jews		Protestants		Catholics	
Parenthood of 1964 Marrieds	1961 Apostasy	1964 Apostasy	1961 Apostasy	1964 Apostasy	1961 Apostasy	1964 Apostasy
Without children	13	11 (503)	11	12 (2,658)	9	13 (556)
With children	8	7 (638)	8	8 (4,683)	5	6 (1,921)

Having children turned out to be a strong deterrent to apostasy in each religion in both 1961 and 1964. This can be seen by reading down the columns in each religious group. The rows of Table 7.10 are also of some interest. Among Jews, whether or not children were present in the family, the trend was toward returning to the fold. Among childless Protestants apostasy increased by a mere percentage point, and it remained fixed at 8 percent among the Protestants with children. The picture was quite different among Catholics, the group, we have seen, that took apostasy seriously and tended to move toward apostasy over time. This trend was especially typical of the childless married Catholics, as their rate of apostasy increased from 9 to 13 percent over the three-year period. But among

Catholics with children, the overall apostasy rates were significantly lower, and the trend from 1961 to 1964 was an increase of only one percentage point. Thus, among Catholics, children had a deterrent effect on apostasy.

The import of Table 7.10 is that married couples with children are much more inclined to retain their religious identity than married couples without children. This reinforces a theme encountered earlier when we examined the impact of quality of parental relations on apostasy. The family obviously has an impact on apostasy. Just as respondents who enjoyed good relations with their parents were more likely to retain a religious identity, so now we learn that respondents who had embarked on a family of their own–with all the responsibilities of parenthood–were also more likely to retain their religious identity.

We have seen that changes in marital status had little impact on the dynamics of apostasy while having children reinforced identification. But one aspect of marriage had a pronounced impact on apostasy: whether one marries a co-religionist or someone raised in a different religion. The most dramatic impact on the dynamics of apostasy is found when the variable of endogamous vs. exogamous marriage is examined. Table 7.11 shows the trend data over the three-year period for those who married a co-religionist and those who married someone raised in a religion other than their own.

Table 7.11: 1961 and 1964 Apostasy Rates of Married Respondents According to Whether They Married Endogamously or Exogamously (in percentages)

	Jews		Protestants		Catholics	
Type of Marriage	1961 Apostasy	1964 Apostasy	1961 Apostasy	1964 Apostasy	1961 Apostasy	1964 Apostasy
Endogamous	7	5 (1,087)	7	7 (6,668)	3	3 (1,792)
Exogamous	40	44 (128)	24	28 (974)	18	23 (693)

The role that intermarriage plays in apostasy is evident from the columns of Table 7.11. From four to five times as many apostates are found among those who intermarried as among those who married endogamously. Intermarriage also contributes to a trend toward apostasy. In every religion the intermarriers were more likely to be apostates in 1964 than in 1961, whereas those who married a co-religionist did not manifest this trend, their apostasy rates in 1964 being much the same as in 1961.

The impact of intermarriage on generating and preserving apostasy becomes even clearer when we examine Table 7.12, which shows the impact of intermarriage on those who were initially (1961) identifiers and apostates.

Table 7.12: Proportion of 1961 Identifiers and Apostates Who Became Apostates or Remained Apostates in 1964 by Type of Marriage (in percentages)

Type of Marriage	1961 Identifiers Who Became Apostates in 1964	1961 Apostates Who Remained Apostates in 1964
Jews		
Endogamous	2 (1,006)	32 (81)
Exogamous	18 (77)	84 (51)
Protestants		
Endogamous	3 (6,169)	55 (499)
Exogamous	11 (745)	80 (229)
Catholics		
Endogamous	1 (1,742)	58 (50)
Exogamous	9 (567)	87 (126)

The upper-left-hand percentage in each part of Table 7.12 refers to the proportion of original identifiers who married endogamously and switched to apostasy. As the figures show, this hardly ever happened as only 2 percent of the vast number of Jewish identifiers who married a co-religionist had opted for apostasy in 1964, 3 percent of the Protestants, and a mere one percent of the Catholics. Clearly, marrying within one's religion has a strong preserving effect on religious identity. But what happens when an initial identifier marries outside his religion? The data show that these people were much more susceptible to apostasy than their counterparts who married within the religious group. Thus, among Jews, 18 percent of the original identifiers who intermarried ended up apostates; among Protestants, 11 percent did; and among Catholics, the figure was 9 percent. Although these proportions are significantly larger than those for the identifiers who married endogamously, they are still quite small. In each religion, the overwhelming majority of the original identifiers continued to identify with their religion of origin even when they did intermarry.

The preserving and generating effects of type of marriage are quite striking when we examine those in each religion who were apostates in 1961. In each religion, especially the Jews, apostates who married endogamously showed a strong tendency to reassume their religious identity. Among initial Jewish apostates who married a co-religionist, a substantial majority (68 percent) returned to the fold; out of the Protestant apostates who married Protestants, 45 percent gave up their apostasy; and among Catholics 42 percent of the apostates who married a fellow Catholic reaffirmed their Catholicism. But intermarriage had a powerful preserving effect among apostates in each religion. Fully 84 percent of the Jewish apostates who intermarried remained apostates in 1964; and 80 percent of the Protestants did; among Catholics the figure was 87 percent. The base figures in Table 7.12 are also of some interest. It will be noted that among the 1961 apostates who were raised as Jews or Protestants (the second column), a majority married endogamously. (See base figures.) But initial Catholic apostates showed a strong preference for exogamous marriages. This is yet another clue to the more serious and permanent nature of Catholic apostasy. Catholics, when compared with Jews and Protestants, experience the least amount of apostasy. But when Catholics do apostatize, they are much less likely to return, and they are much more likely to tie their decision to intermarriage.

The analysis of the impact of intermarriage on the dynamics of apostasy brings to a close our examination of the determinants of trends and turnover in religious status. We have seen that the "germs" of apostasy, identified in the analysis of the

1961 data, affected apostasy in 1964, and that changes in the "germs" resulted in corresponding changes in religious status. The last part of the chapter examined the role of intervening events in the dynamics of apostasy and we noted that type of postgraduate education, type of postgraduate employment, parenthood, and intermarriage all had significant impacts on shifts in religious status.

This analysis of the dynamics of apostasy has shown, for the first time, a sharp difference among the three religious groups. The preceding chapters, which examined "germs" of apostasy at the time of graduation, showed that whatever trait produced apostasy in one of the major religious groups had the same effect in the others. But the study of the dynamics of apostasy had demonstrated that the Jews differ sharply from the Protestants and the Catholics. In brief, the analysis disclosed two characteristics of Jewish apostasy that do not apply to the Christian religions. First, the Jews showed a tendency over the three-year period to return to the fold, that is, more Jews gave up apostasy over the three year period than opted for apostasy. In contrast, both the Protestants and Catholics demonstrated a trend toward apostasy, as in each of these religions there were more apostates in the sample in 1964 than in 1961. Second, independent of the trend data, the Jewish apostates of 1961 turned out to be highly unstable, as many more of them relinquished their apostasy than did Protestant and, particularly, Catholic apostates. Although Jews had the highest apostasy rate in 1961, ever so slightly higher than the Protestant rate, and substantially higher than the Catholic rate, the Catholic apostates proved to be the staunchest—the most committed to their position. The Protestants in this respect finished second.

What are the implications of these findings? Although the definitive data are not at hand to test our interpretation, we would like to suggest that these findings point to the greater power of the secularization process in America than to the power of the values of modernization—i.e., universalism and achievement as opposed to particularism and ascription. As we have noted throughout this study, Jewish identity, to a much greater extent than Protestant identity and, in particular, Catholic identity, rests upon communality (ethnicity) rather than upon religiosity. In contrast, Protestant identity and, in particular, Catholic identity rest upon religiosity, i.e., belief in the dogmas of the religion. The greater stability of the apostasy of Protestants and Catholics and the trend toward apostasy in these religions can be interpreted by the process of secularization, i.e., the undermining of religious belief in modern society. That the patterns for the Jews are quite different can be explained by the fact that Jewish identity, much more than Protestant or Catholic identity, rests upon communality rather than religiosity. It has become quite fashionable in the seventies to point to the persistence of ethnic ties in defiance of the "melting-pot" hypothesis. Within the past five years, dozens of scholarly articles have been written about the "white ethnics" and the strength of ethnicity in America today. That the "turnover" picture regarding religious identity was markedly different for Jews than for Christians can perhaps best be explained by the strength of ethnicity in America today, an appeal that is delaying and retarding the adoption of the values of the intellectuals–universalism and achievement. In short, Protestants and Catholics demonstrate a trend toward apostasy because the basis for their religious identification–religiosity–has suffered greatly in the 20th century. But the Jews are still able to maintain the loyalties of their sons and daughters who have been exposed to a college education because of the communal, as distinct from religious, basis for such an identification.

NOTES

1. For an exposition of panel analysis, see Bernard Levenson, "Panel Analysis," *Encyclopedia of the Social Sciences,* New York: Macmillan, 1967; and P.F. Lazarsfeld, A.K. Pasanella, and M. Rosenberg, *Continuities in the Language of Social Research,* New York: Free Press, 1971, Section IV.

2. It will be recalled that quality of parental relations was measured only at time 2 (1964). We will treat it, however, as if it were measured at time 1 (1961) on the grounds that these reports of early childhood experience were more or less constant by the time the seniors were ready to graduate from college.

Chapter 8

UPDATING APOSTASY

A serious criticism of the preceding chapters is that they are based on data that may well be out of date. Some fifteen years have passed since the first wave of the NORC panel study of 1961 college graduates. Apostasy rates may have increased or decreased since then, and the correlates of apostasy may have changed. This chapter turns to newer sources of data in order to update the picture of apostasy among those who have gone to college. This updating is based on three sets of data. In 1968, after a gap of four years, NORC administered a fifth wave to a subsample of 5000 of the original respondents from the class of 1961. As in the earlier waves, the respondents were asked about current religion, an item that could be related to their report of original religion in the earlier waves. We are thus able to study trends in apostasy among the 1961 cohort over a period of seven years from 1961 to 1968.

The second source of information on apostasy among college students consists of a massive survey of undergraduates,

graduates, and faculty members conducted by the American Council on Education on behalf of the Carnegie Foundation in 1969. We have already reported the rates of apostasy among the faculty members in this study in Chapter 4; we shall now consider the apostasy of the undergraduates and graduates as of 1969. As we shall see, the Carnegie study permits us to provide a direct answer to the question raised in Chapter 6, the role of the college in generating apostasy.

A third source of apostasy data consists of the annual surveys of entering college freshmen conducted by the American Council on Education. These surveys, which began in 1966, permit us to examine trends in apostasy among those entering college over a decade.

Trends in Apostasy: The Picture Seven Years after Graduation

The previous chapter examined trends in apostasy between 1961 and 1964. We saw that in this period apostasy declined slightly among Jews (from 13 to 12 percent), while it remained constant among Protestants (11 percent), and increased among Catholics (from 6 to 8 percent). The divergence of the Jews from the pattern of the Protestants and Catholics was one of the few instances in which results have differed from one religious group to the others. On the basis of the fifth wave, administered to a subsample of 5000 cases in 1968, it can be seen that the 1961-64 trends continued over the next four years.

Table 8.1 shows the apostasy rates for each religion from 1961 through 1968 in the subsample of 5000. (Table 8.1 is based on the weighted sample.)

Table 8.1: Trends in Apostasy by Religion of Origin: 1961-1964-1968 (percentage apostates)

Religion of Origin	1961	1964	1968	N
Jews	10	11	8	(537)
Protestants	11	12	17	(4,662)
Catholics	5	8	10	(1,735)

Jewish and Catholic apostates as of 1961 were less likely than identifiers to participate in the fifth wave of the survey in 1968. Whereas 13 percent of the Jews in the complete sample were apostates in 1961 and 12 percent in 1964, only 10 percent of the Jews in the subsample of 1968 were apostates in 1961, a figure that increased to 11 percent in 1964 even though in the full sample Jews showed a slight decline. The full sample showed the apostasy rate among Protestants to be constant from 1961 to 1964, but in this subsample the Protestant rate increased by one percentage point, from 11 to 12 percent. Finally, Catholics in the full sample showed a two percentage-point increase in apostasy from 1961 to 1964, but in the subsample the 1961 to 1964 increase was three percentage points, from 5 to 8 percent.

These discrepancies between the full sample and the subsample are much less significant than the trends over the eight year period shown by the 1968 subsample. The critical data in Table 8.1 are those identifying trends in apostasy between 1964 and 1968. Among Jews, apostasy declined by two percentage points over this period, in keeping with the results for the entire sample of Jews over the 1961-1964 period. In contrast to the Jews, the Protestants showed a sharp increase in apostasy from 1964 to 1968, from 12 to 17 percent, approximately a 40 percent increase. And among Catholics, apostasy continued to increase to the point where, in this subsample, the 1968 rate was exactly double the 1961 rate.

The decline in apostasy among Jews over the time period under analysis and the increase in apostasy among Protestants and Catholics is in keeping with the different bases of identification in these religions. Because Jewish identity rests as much on communality as on religiosity, Jews who returned to the broader community after college no doubt experienced pressures to retain their religious identity. In contrast, Protestants and Catholics, for whom identity is primarily a matter of religiosity, continued to be exposed to secularizing forces that undermined religious commitment and, hence their apostasy continued to grow in the years following college.

A more complete picture of changes in religious status over the seven-year period is provided by relating religious status at time 1 to religious status at time 2, permiting us to study "turnover." This is done in Table 8.2.

Table 8.2: Turnover in Religious Status (1961-1964), (1964-68), and (1961-68) (in percentages, based on weighted samples)

		1968 Subsample		
		1961-64	1964-68	1961-68
Jews				
T1	*T2*			
Identifier	identifier	86	87	85
Identifier	apostate	4	3	5
Apostate	identifier	4	6	7
Apostate	apostate	6	4	3
		100	100	100
		(451)	(447)	(442)
Protestants				
T1	*T2*			
Identifier	identifier	85	82	80
Identifier	apostate	4	7	9
Apostate	identifier	4	2	4
Apostate	apostate	7	9	7
		100	100	100
		(2,631)	(2,549)	(2,434)
Catholics				
T1	*T2*			
Identifier	identifier	93	89	90
Identifier	apostate	3	4	5
Apostate	identifier	1	1	1
Apostate	apostate	3	6	4
		100	100	100
		(1,033)	(1,018)	(1,011)

From the top third of the table, we see that between 1961 and 1964 as many Jews left the fold as returned (4 percent changing in each direction), but over the next four years twice as many Jews gave up their apostasy and returned to the group as left it (6 percent compared with 3 percent). But if Jews manifested the pattern of returning to the fold, Protestants and Catholics showed a consistent trend away from their religion of origin and toward apostasy. For Protestants, between 1964 and

1968 more than three times as many gave up their religious identification for apostasy as gave up their apostasy to rejoin the group (7 percent compared with 2 percent). And the pattern of leaving the fold was even more pronounced among Catholics. In both the 1961-1964 and 1964-1968 periods hardly any Catholics gave up their apostasy, but 3 percent and 4 percent gave up their affiliation and joined the apostates. Among both Protestants and Catholics, the number of consistent identifiers declined over the eight-year period, whereas among Jews consistent identifiers were as frequent in the later period as in the earlier one. The data from the 1968 subsample thus confirm the picture that emerged in the previous chapter of the dynamics of apostasy over the 1961-1964 period. Among Jews, apostasy does not increase; rather, Jewish apostates show a pattern of returning to the fold. In contrast, among both Protestants and Catholics, apostasy increases over time.

College Apostasy in 1969: The Carnegie Study

The Carnegie Foundation's survey of undergraduates and graduate students in 1969 opens several vistas for our study. First, the Carnegie data permit updating apostasy among college graduates by showing the amount of apostasy eight years after the portrait provided in the previous chapters. Second, the Carnegie study allows an examination of the germs of apostasy at a later point. If the traits shown to be related to apostasy in 1961 were related to apostasy in 1969, we can have considerable confidence in the causal model of apostasy that has been developed. Finally, the Carnegie data provide a direct measure of the impact of college on apostasy. In Chapter 6 we analyzed the static 1961 data in such a way that we could make inferences about the role of the college in generating apostasy. But the 1961 data dealt only with college seniors. The 1969 Carnegie study provides data on students in each year of college but, more importantly, because of the unique sampling design of this study, we know whether these students were apostates or identifiers before they started college. This panel design results from the fact that the undergraduates in the Carnegie study were sampled from those who completed the annual questionnaires administered to incoming freshmen by the American Council on Education. In short, for the undergraduates in the Carnegie study, we know their religion of origin and their religious affiliation at the outset of college and also after one or more years of college.[1]

As in the presentation of the NORC data, we shall use the *weighted* samples to report the absolute amounts of apostasy in each religion and the *unweighted* samples to analyze the correlates of apostasy. As explained earlier this is justified, for in examining correlates we are concerned not with the absolute amount of apostasy but rather with the strength of relationships, and one can be certain that relationships uncovered by the unweighted sample will hold for the weighted sample as well.

A comparison of college seniors in 1969 with seniors in 1961 shows a sharp increase in apostasy in each religion. As we have noted, in 1961 Jewish college seniors had an apostasy rate of 13 percent. Eight years later the Jewish rate had climbed to 21 percent. The Protestant rate in 1961 was 12 percent and in 1969 17 percent. The most dramatic increase in apostasy took place among Catholics. From a 1961 rate of only 7 percent it grew to 19 percent by 1969, an increase of fully 171 percent. The picture of protected Catholics who adhere to their religion to a much greater extent than Jews and Protestants presented by the NORC data is totally obliterated in the Carnegie data. By 1969 Catholic apostasy more than matched the apostasy rate of Protestants and came close to the Jewish rate.

CATHOLIC APOSTASY

This key finding with respect to the Catholics no doubt reflects the demise of the Catholic college as the protector of the faith among Catholic college students. The eight year period following the NORC study had witnessed both the secularization of Catholic colleges as they loosened their religious commitment and the rejection of Catholic colleges in favor of secular institutions by Catholics seeking a higher education.

The decline of the Catholic college as the bastion against secular society is domonstrated by both the annual surveys of incoming freshmen conducted by the American Council on Education and the Carnegie study of 1969. According to the NORC survey of 1961, 25 percent of college seniors at that time were Catholics and fully 42 percent of these were attending Catholic colleges. In the interval two significant trends developed. First, the number of Catholics attending college increased significantly. By 1966, Catholics comprised 28 percent of the entering freshmen, a figure that steadily grew to 36 percent by 1974 (an increase of 44 percent since 1961). Even more significantly, the proportion of Catholics attending Catholic colleges has declined sharply over this period. Whereas 42 percent of the NORC Catholics (who had started college in 1957) attended Catholic colleges, the American Council on Education's survey of entering freshmen in 1966 showed that in that year 26 percent of the Catholics were enrolled in Catholic colleges. By 1969 this figure had decreased still further to 15 percent, and by 1974 Catholic freshmen attending Catholic colleges had shrunk to a mere 7 percent. Incredibly enough, in a span of 15 years Catholic enrollment in Catholic colleges declined by 35 percentage points (from 42 to 7 percent). The breakdown of the Catholic college as a home for Catholic college students is undoubtedly a major reason for the sharp rise in Catholic apostasy. But the movement of Catholics to nondenominational schools is only part of the story. Also important are the forces that have brought about a secularization of the Catholic colleges. In Table 6.2 we saw that it was sufficient for a Catholic to attend a Catholic college to insure his retaining the faith, for only 1 percent of the Catholics at Catholic colleges among the 1961 seniors apostatized. But this protective shield from apostasy provided by the Catholic college in 1961 had broken down by 1969. Among Catholic undergraduates in that year, apostasy was about as likely to occur among those attending Catholic colleges as among those in nondenominational schools. This can be seen from Table 8.3. (The relatively few Catholics attending Protestant colleges are omitted from this table, although they tended to have the highest apostasy rates, a fact that may reflect the small case base.)

Table 8.3: Apostasy Rates of Catholics by Year in College Presented Separately for Catholic Colleges and Nondenominational Colleges (1969) (Weighted Samples, in percentages)*

Year in College	Catholic College	Nondenominational College
Senior	13 (11,008)	21 (43,170)
Junior	17 (10,191)	16 (41,252)
Sophomore	11 (11,474)	12 (57,470)
Freshman	9 (13,608)	9 (52,976)

*It should be noted that the N's that appear in the parentheses in this table are the result of the weights and do not reflect actual respondents. All the weighted tables based on the Carnegie study were generated from a subsample data type of 20,000 cases or roughly 5000 in each year of college.

When compared with Table 6.2, Table 8.3 is quite startling. Only among the 1969 seniors did attendance at a Catholic college seem to have a deterrent effect on apostasy, 13 percent compared with 21 percent, but the apostasy rate among seniors at Catholic colleges was extremely high compared with the mere 1 percent in 1961. Among the juniors, sophomores, and freshmen, attendence at a Catholic college did nothing to inhibit apostasy among Catholics, for the rates at the Catholic colleges were virtually identical to those found at the nondenominational schools.

The effort of the Catholic community to develop parallel institutions to meet the needs of its members and still retain their allegiance appears to have failed in the sixties. This was, of course, the decade of considerable turmoil in American society as a result of the Vietnam war and the civil rights movement, the decade that saw student protest bring higher education virtually to a halt. Whether the Catholic college's waning influence over its flock has stemmed from inexorable forces of secularization or whether it became somehow a victim of the Vietnam war is not clear. But the data do show quite clearly that the Catholic college is no longer performing the function it once did of keeping the college-educated Catholics within the fold.

The Germs of Apostasy Revisited

An assumption of the analysis of the previous chapters has been that whatever the *rate* of apostasy over time, the determinants and correlates of apostasy developed on the basis of the 1961 data are more or less enduring. In short, we have assumed that the traits that have been identified as causes of apostasy transcend any particular time. This assumption can now be tested with the 1969 Carnegie data, for that study contains indicators of the various "germs" of apostasy identified earlier.

QUALITY OF PARENTAL RELATIONS

The respondents in the Carnegie study were asked a battery of questions, much like those asked of the 1961 seniors in the NORC study, tapping degree of closeness to mother and father in a variety of situations. On the basis of these questions, we have constructed an index of quality of parental relations, an index trichotomized into three categories, "good," "fair," and "poor."[2] Table 8.4 shows that quality of parental relations is related to apostasy in each religion among 1969 seniors as was the case among 1961 seniors.

Table 8.4: Apostasy by Quality of Parental Relations in Each Religion of Origin (1969), (in percentages)

Religion of Origin	Quality of Parental Relations		
	Good	Fair	Poor
Jewish	15 (673)	25 (566)	31 (316)
Protestant	15 (4,653)	23 (3,835)	32 (2,145)
Catholic	12 (2,085)	21 (2,017)	29 (1,265)

As quality of parental relations worsened apostasy increased in each religion. The one difference between this finding and the comparable one based on the class of 1961 is that the pattern is as pronounced among Catholics as among the other religions. This is in keeping with the finding of Table 8.3 showing that the relative immunity to apostasy among Catholics evident in 1961 had broken down by 1969.

POLITICAL ORIENTATION

Political orientation was found to be a major correlate of apostasy, but the NORC study lacked a clear indicator of the left-right continuum. This deficiency is corrected in the Carnegie study. The political question asked the respondents to identify themselves in one of four categories, conservative, middle-of-the-road, liberal, or left. Thus, unlike the NORC study, the Carnegie study provided for a position more extreme than liberal. That political orientation is an important factor in apostasy can be seen from Table 8.5.

Table 8.5: Apostasy by Political Orientation in Each Religion of Origin (1969), (in percentages)

Religion of Origin	Political Orientation			
	Conservative	Middle-of-Road	Liberal	Left
Jewish	18 (97)	10 (222)	18 (846)	40 (357)
Protestant	8 (2,081)	10 (3,104)	29 (4,446)	53 (842)
Catholic	8 (795)	9 (1,609)	24 (2,502)	59 (372)

The base figures of Table 8.5 show marked differences in the political orientations of the three religious groups. Although "liberal" is the modal response in each religion, this description is far more characteristic of Jews than of Protestants and Catholics. The Protestants are the most conservative in that half identify themselves as either middle-of-the-roaders or conservatives as do 46 percent of the Catholics, in contrast with only 21 percent of the Jews. Jews are much more likely than Protestants and Catholics to describe themselves as leftists (23 percent compared with 8 percent and 7 percent). The connection between political orientation and apostasy is shown by the rows of Table 8.5. Among both Protestants and Catholics, apostasy steadily increases with the shift from right to left on the political spectrum. Whereas less than 10 percent of the conservatives in these religions are apostates, more than half of those who identify with the left are apostates. Among Jews, the critical difference is between those on the far left and those with less extreme political orientations. The substantial minority of Jews who identify with the left are much more likely to apostatize than other Jews although their rate of 40 percent does not match that of the leftist Christians.[3] Table 8.5 thus confirms the role of political orientation in generating apostasy suggested by the NORC data of 1961.

INTELLECTUALISM

The NORC data showed that graduates committed to an intellectual way of life were much more prone to apostasy than those who were not so oriented. The Carnegie study provides two indicators of intellectualism, the degree to which the self-description of intellectual was judged to be appropriate by the respondent and whether the 1969 graduate was oriented toward the home of intellectuals, academia, as a career site. The undergraduates in the Carnegie study were asked a Likert scale question, ranging from agree strongly to disagree strongly regarding the self-description "intellectual," which we have trichotomized as representing low, medium, and high commitment to intellectuality. Among Jews, apostasy increased from 18 percent of those low on intellectuality to 27 percent of those who were high. For Protestants the comparable figures were 16 and 32 percent, and for Catholics apostasy increased with intellectuality from 14 to 35 percent. As these data show, the highly intellectual Protestants and Catholics were even more prone to apostasy than their Jewish counterparts.

The other indicator of intellectual commitment in the Carnegie study was the career orientation of the college senior, namely the sector of the occupational structure to which he was oriented. The impact of career orientation on apostasy is shown in Table 8.6. In each religion, those oriented toward academia were most likely to apostatize and those oriented toward school teaching were least likely to. The public schools are very much enmeshed in the local community in which the religious spirit burns brightly in America and hence it is not too surprising that those who planned to work in public schools were most ready to retain their religious commitment. The key point of Table 8.6 is

Table 8.6: Apostasy by Career Orientation in Each Religion of Origin (1969), (in percentages)

Career Orientation	Jews	Protestants	Catholics
Academia (professoriate)	28 (260)	32 (1,275)	32 (578)
Nonprofit private sector	23 (285)	24 (2,058)	22 (988)
Professionals	17 (370)	24 (1,542)	24 (730)
Business	20 (240)	19 (2,104)	17 (1,098)
Government	18 (67)	18 (2,104)	17 (366)
School teaching	18 (176)	13 (2,034)	12 (1,058)

that those choosing the most intellectual career, college teaching, were most prone to apostasy. These data confirm the significance of another apostasy germ, intellectualism.

RELIGIOSITY

Remaining to be considered is the most powerful of all apostasy germs, the loss of religious faith. The Carnegie study provides information on two indicators of religiosity, a question asking students to indicate how religious they are and another asking them whether they believe in God.

The Carnegie respondents could agree strongly, agree with reservations, disagree with reservations, or disagree strongly with the statement, "I consider myself religious." Those who disagreed strongly were treated as low on religiosity, those who disagreed with reservations, as medium, and those who agreed strongly or with reservations, as high on religiosity. Table 8.7 shows how religiosity was related to apostasy in each religion among college seniors in 1969.

Table 8.7: Apostasy by Religiosity in Each Religion of Origin (1969), (in percentages)

Religion of Origin	Religiosity		
	Low	Medium	High
Jews	39 (604)	14 (432)	10 (400)
Protestants	67 (1,936)	26 (2,334)	6 (5,153)
Catholics	69 (845)	25 (1,153)	6 (2,929)

In each religion, apostasy increases sharply as religiosity diminishes. This pattern is particularly true of the Protestants and Catholics but much less so of the Jews who, as we have noted time and again, rest their religious identification more on communality than on religiosity. Among the Protestants and Catholics who are not at all religious, a substantial majority are apostates, but among the nonreligious Jews, although apostasy is most marked, a substantial majority are nonetheless identifiers. The base figures of Table 8.7 are quite revealing for they show a marked difference in religiosity among the three religions. A substantial majority of both Protestants and Catholics falls into the high-religiosity category, but only a small minority of the Jews is high on religiosity. This is yet another sign of the greater prevalence of apostasy germs among Jews and, in spite of this prevalence, of the resistance of Jews to apostasy. The base figures of Table 8.7 are significant in another respect. They show a decline in religiosity among college seniors, particularly the Catholics, between 1961 and 1969. This loss of faith is part of the process whereby Catholics have caught up with Jews and Protestants with regard to apostasy.

Another respect in which there were marked differences between the three religions was on the issue of belief in God. Only 27 percent of the Jewish students in the Carnegie study said they believed in God. In contrast, 58 percent of the Protestant students were believers and fully 75 percent of the Catholic students were. This belief turned out to be a strong deterrent to apostasy. Only 5 percent of the Jewish believers were apostates compared with 29 percent of the nonbelievers. Among Protestants only 4 percent of the believers were apostates, compared with 44 percent of those who did not believe in God, and among Catholics these figures were 6 and 57 percent. Again, we find an apostasy germ having a much greater impact among Protestants and Catholics than among Jews.

The data presented in this section lend substance to the forces leading to apostasy found on the basis of the 1961 data. The various germs identified earlier are by no means time bound. They were as significant in 1969 as they were in 1961, indicating that they are enduring determinants of apostasy.

Apostasy Among Graduate Students in 1969

Chapter 4 demonstrated a strong link between intellectualism and apostasy, a link reaffirmed by the 1969 data on college seniors. We saw that students attracted to intellectual careers were much more likely to apostatize than those not so attracted and that college professors, those most committed to intellectual careers, were even more prone to apostasy than college seniors oriented toward the intellectual life. The path to an academic career inevitably involves graduate study, the pursuit of the Ph.D. degree. If intellectualism is indeed a force leading to apostasy, then graduate students, particularly those pursuing the Ph.D. degree, the passport to academic employment, should be much more prone to apostasy than college seniors. The graduate data from the Carnegie study show this to be the case. It is a moot point whether the weighted or unweighted samples should be used for this purpose, but since we are interested mainly in the relationship between graduate status and apostasy, rather than in the absolute amount of apostasy, we present in Table 8.8 the apostasy rates of 1969 college seniors, 1969 graduate students pursuing professional degrees, and 1969 graduate students pursuing Ph.D. degrees based on the unweighted samples.

Table 8.8: Apostasy Rates for 1969 College Seniors, Graduate Students Pursuing Professional Degrees and Graduate Students Pursuing the Ph.D. Degree (unweighted samples, in percentages)*

Cohort	Jews	Protestants	Catholics
1969 College seniors	23	22	20
1969 Graduates in professions	18	23	18
1969 Graduate Ph.D. candidates	27	36	29

*The unweighted apostasy rate for Jews among the 1969 seniors is two percentage points greater than the weighted rate; for Catholics it is one percentage point larger; but for Protestants the unweighted rate (22 percent) is five percentage points higher than the weighted rate (17 percent).

A comparison of the first and second rows of Table 8.8 indicates that graduates seeking to become professionals, e.g., doctors, lawyers, teachers, etc., were no more likely than college seniors to apostatize; in fact, among Jews and Catholics, seniors were somewhat more likely to apostatize than those oriented toward the professions. This finding is not too surprising because professionals are oriented toward the broader community whose needs they will serve, and professionals cannot afford to be too far out of step with their clients. Table 8.6 showed the apostasy rates of seniors who were oriented toward the professions. It is of some interest that the apostasy rates for those who had not yet begun their professional training were quite similar to those of the people already in professional school. Professional school is clearly not an environment generating new apostates. But the same cannot be said for graduate school, the environment in which students aspire to the Ph.D. degree. As the last row of Table 8.8 makes clear, apostasy increases in each religion among those pursuing Ph.D.s. The pattern is relatively slight for the Jews, quite evident among the Catholics and particularly pronounced among the Protestants. The apostasy rates of Ph.D. candidates tend to fall in between those of intellectual college seniors and the faculty at high-quality institutions, in keeping with a notion of career development of intellectuality as a cause of apostasy.

THE IMPACT OF COLLEGE ON APOSTASY

Chapter 6 confronted the question of the role of college in generating apostasy. It seemed plausible that the college experience with its stress on scientific truths would help undermine religious commitment and contribute to apostasy, but since we only had data on college seniors at the point at which they were about to graduate from college, we could not demonstrate conclusively that college did contribute to apostasy. Through an elaborate process of inference we did conclude that the college experience played a causal role in the development of apostasy. The data of the Carnegie study permit us to confront directly the issue of the impact of the college experience. There are two aspects of the Carnegie study that make a direct test of the role of the college possible. First, the Carnegie study dealt with undergraduates on all levels, not merely seniors. Thus, by comparing the apostasy rates of freshmen, sophomores, juniors and seniors, we can see if trends in apostasy occur over the four year sequence of college. There is one flaw in this procedure, however. It assumes that the rate of apostasy at the start of college was fairly constant. But the apostasy rates of the entering freshmen may have increased or decreased over the four-year period. If they increased, then differences produced by the college experience would be muted in the comparisons between students in different classes. If, for some reason, apostasy declined among the entering freshmen from one year to the next, then class comparisons would exaggerate the impact of college on apostasy.

Fortunately, we do not have to rely only on the interclass comparisons to assess the impact of college. The Carnegie study incorporated the panel design in that the 1969 samples of undergraduates were drawn from lists of students who had participated in the American Council on Education's annual surveys of entering freshmen. The entering freshmen were asked the two religion questions, and so it is possible to compare the amount of apostasy among these students at the start of their college career with the amount of apostasy they manifested after being in college for one, two, three, or four years. These panel data provide a definitive answer to the question of whether apostasy increases during the college experience. Since we are concerned with the absolute amount of apostasy at different times, we shall base this analysis on the *weighted* sample.

Table 8.9 shows the apostasy rates in each religion of freshmen, sophomores, juniors, and seniors as of 1969 and the start of college. This table is rich in information. The first column tells us whether there was a trend toward apostasy through the college years. the Jews and Catholics demonstrate a modest trend toward apostasy, but among the Protestants the apostasy

Table 8.9: Apostasy by Year in College and at the Start of College by Religion of Origin (Weighted Sample), (1969), (in percentages)

Religion of Origin	Apostasy as of 1969	Apostasy at Start of College	Difference
Jews			
Freshmen	12	15	-3
Sophomore	16	15	+1
Juniors	22	10	+12
Seniors	21	13	+8
Protestants			
Freshmen	15	14	+1
Sophomores	17	9	+8
Juniors	17	7	+10
Seniors	17	7	+10
Catholics			
Freshmen	10	13	-3
Sophomores	14	6	+8
Juniors	16	6	+10
Seniors	19	3	+16

rate is quite constant among those at different stages of college. The second column shows trends toward apostasy among successive classes of freshmen. Jewish freshmen over this four-year period show only a slight trend toward apostasy as the current freshmen and sophomores were slightly more likely to be apostates at the start of college than the Jewish juniors and seniors. A trend toward apostasy is more evident among the Protestant and Catholic entering freshmen over this four-year period. Among both Protestants and Catholics, the current freshmen were much more likely to have been apostates at the start of college than the Protestant and Catholic upperclassmen. The data bearing on the impact of college on apostasy appears in the third column of Table 8.9, which shows the difference in the apostasy rates at the start of college and after one or more years of college. In each religion the difference between apostasy at the start of college and after a given year of college is substantially greater among the upperclassmen who have been in college for three or four years. Among Jews, there is little difference in the apostasy rates of freshmen and sophomores from the beginning of college to the end of their freshmen or sophomore year. But among juniors and seniors, apostasy among Jews increases substantially over the entrance rates. A similar pattern is found among Protestants. They seem to be influenced by college at an even earlier level than the Jews, for apostasy among Protestants substantially increases after the sophomore year and continues to grow after the junior and senior years. The most telling case for the impact of college on apostasy is found in the patterns for the Catholics. After the freshman year of college, apostasy among Catholics decreases somewhat over what it was at the beginning of college. But after two years in college, apostasy in the sophomore cohort of Catholics increases by 8 percentage points; after the junior year, Catholic apostasy grows by 10 percentage points; and after the senior year by fully 16. The patterns for the Catholics and somewhat less so for the Protestants and Jews clearly indicate that the college experience generates apostasy. The more years spent in college, the greater the loss to the religion of origin.

The Trend Toward Apostasy Among Entering Freshmen

Table 8.9 suggested that between 1965 and 1969 those starting college were more and more likely to be apostates. This finding confirms the trend toward apostasy shown by the comparison of the 1961 and 1969 seniors. Even before the impact of college can be felt, apostasy is apparently increasing among those headed toward higher education. The annual surveys of entering freshmen by the American Council on Education provide a dramatic demonstration of this trend. From 1966 to 1972, with the exception of 1970, the ACE surveys inquired about religion reared in and current religion. In 1970 and from 1973 on, the surveys asked for the religion of mother and father rather than religion raised in. Table 8.10 shows the results for 1966, 1968 and 1972, years in which the respondents were asked about religion raised in and current religion.

The breakdown of religious identity over time is shown by the trend toward apostasy in each religion over this period. The pattern is somewhat different in each religion. The Jewish

Table 8.10: Trends in Religious Status in Each Religion of Origin at the Start of College (1966-1976), (in percentages)

	1966	1968	1972
Jews			
Identifiers	91	83	82
Converts	1	3	3
Apostates	8	14	15
	100	100	100
Protestants			
Identifiers	90	88	81
Converts	4	4	5
Apostates	7	8	14
	101	100	100
Catholics			
Identifiers	94	91	82
Converts	2	2	4
Apostates	4	7	14
	100	100	100

apostasy rate increased markedly between 1966 and 1968 but then leveled off over the next four years. The Catholic rate steadily increased, jumping sharply in 1972. The Protestant rate did not increase until after 1968, when it too climbed significantly.

Table 8.10 demonstrates that the breakdown of the constraints against apostasy among Catholics occurs prior to the college experience. Even before being exposed to the secularizing forces of college, Catholics starting college in 1972 had caught up with Jews and Protestants regarding apostasy. Apparently the constraints against apostasy for young Catholics operative in the family and high schools had begun to break down by 1972. Whereas the NORC data showed that it took exposure to a high-quality Ivy League school for the Catholic senior in 1961 to become vulnerable to apostasy, the Carnegie and ACE data show that by the late sixties and early seventies, this vulnerability was evident among Catholics before they started their college careers.

Apostasy among entering freshmen apparently peaked in 1972. The data for subsequent years show a decline in the percentage reporting "no religion" at the time they entered college. In 1972, this figure was 16 percent; by 1974, the apostasy rate had declined to 12 percent and by 1976 to 11 percent. When mother's religion is related to the entering freshmen's religion in 1974 and 1976, the decline in apostasy occurs in every religion. Thus among Jews, 10 percent were, by this measure, apostates in 1974 and 9 percent in 1976; Among Protestants the comparable figures were also 10 and 9 percent, and among Catholics, 7 and 6 percent. Although apostasy among entering freshmen has declined since 1972, the rates as of 1976 were still significantly greater than a decade earlier.

With the ACE data showing the trend toward apostasy among entering freshmen, we bring to a close this effort to update the picture of apostasy among college students and graduates. The portrait of apostasy based on the 1961 and 1964 NORC data is solidly confirmed by the Carnegie and ACE data. All the germs of apostasy identified in 1961 were shown to be significant to apostasy in 1969. We also found that apostasy among college students continued to increase between 1961 and 1960, and judging from the ACE data on incoming freshmen, the progression toward apostasy continues even among those who have not yet been exposed to the college climate. In short, the analysis of more recent data confirms the findings presented in earlier chapters.

NOTES

1. By basing their sample on those who completed questionnaires at the outset of college on any given campus, the Carnegie study is not completely representative of undergraduates in college in 1969. Thus, those who dropped out and later returned are neglected as are the transfer students. But, given the large size of the Carnegie samples, these slight biases are not likely to introduce serious errors. We shall treat the Carnegie samples as if they were representative of undergraduates in 1969.

2. From a battery of items tapping closeness to parents, three were chosen for the purposes of this index: (1) "If I had some kind of problem, I could count on them to help me out," (2) "They comforted me and helped me when I had troubles," and (3) "They made me feel I could talk with them about everything." Students were asked to indicate whether these statements were true or false regarding their father and their mother. These six judgments (two for each item) were combined into the index of quality of parental relations.

3. Oddly enough, the small number of Jews who choose the extreme position of "conservative" have as high an apostasy rate as the "liberal" Jews. These conservative Jews hold to an extremely deviant political orientation in the Jewish community.

Chapter 9

SUMMARY AND CONCLUSIONS

The story of apostasy among college graduates documented in the previous chapters now draws to a close. We began the analysis by noting that a religious identity in America rests on two foundations, a commitment to religious beliefs and practices and a feeling of kinship with a social group united by a common religious tie. In keeping with Lenski, we called the former foundation, religiosity, and the latter, communality or ethnicity. Although the thrust of the analysis was to lay bare the causes of a loss of religious identification, that is, the causes of what we came to call apostasy, perhaps the key finding of the entire study was the discovery that apostasy, at least in 1961, was relatively rare among the highly educated, those most exposed to secularizing forces. Among Jewish and Protestant graduates of 1961, the apostasy rate was 12 percent or so, and among Catholics, a mere 6 percent.

The search for the causes of apostasy focused on the forces undermining the two foundations of religious identity, religious faith and communality. A series of traits were identified as exposing their possessors to apostasy. These included poor parental relations, the symptoms of maladjustment or neurosis, a radical or leftist political orientation, and a commitment to intellectualism and an intellectual career. Each of these traits was found to be related to the others, but through the techniques of multivariate analysis we found that each had some independent effect on apostasy in each religious group. The various determinants of apostasy can be seen as questioning either religiosity or the commitment to social groups based on ascriptive ties. The role of intellectualism perhaps best illustrates this undermining of religious identity.

The most intellectual students, committed to rationality and empiricism, are most likely to question ideas based on articles of faith. Moreover, as we noted throughout the analysis, the more intellectually oriented students can be presumed to be most committed to the modernistic values of universalism and achievement, values that undercut the second basis for a religious identification, a communal tie based on ascription and particularism. Of all the factors related to apostasy, the most significant, not surprisingly, was religious belief. Those in each religion who lost their religious faith for whatever reason were much more likely to relinquish their religious identification than those who still viewed themselves as religious. These generalizations can be presented more precisely by reporting the results of the regression and path analyses that were done linking the determinants to apostasy and to each other.

A Regression Analysis of Apostasy

In the tabular analysis of the preceding chapters, we were only able to examine the impact of a "germ" of apostasy in the light of another "germ," in classic three-variable analysis. The beauty of regression analysis is that it enables us to handle all the independent variables simultaneously, that is, we can examine the net effect of each determinant controlling for the others. In the tabular analysis we presented the results separately for each religion, and a major finding was that what proved to be a determinant of apostasy in one religion also led to apostasy in the others. For this reason, we shall simplify the regression analysis by aggregating the data on the three religions and studying the role of the various germs in generating apostasy for the entire sample of 1961 graduates. This analysis deals with apostasy among the 1961 seniors in the NORC study, the group under analysis in the first six chapters.

Before presenting the results of the path analysis, we shall first deal with the zero order correlations of the germs with the critical intervening variable, religiosity and with apostasy.[1] Among the four apostasy traits of radicalism, intellectualism, maladjustment, and poor parental relations, the strongest correlation is found between radicalism and intellectualism, a Pearsonian R of .22. A close second is the correlation between radicalism and maladjustment (.20). Intellectualism and maladjustment, intellectualism and parental relations, and maladjustment and parental relations all show the same correlation of .13. The lowest correlation among these germs is between intellectualism and parental relations, a correlation of only .08. As these Pearsonian coefficients indicate, the apostasy germs are all related to each other, which is in keeping with the earlier findings based on percentage tables.

Table 9.1 shows the zero order correlations between these four germs and religiosity and the correlations of the germs including religiosity with apostasy.

Table 9.1: The Correlations of Four Germs to Religiosity and to Apostasy and the Correlation of Religiosity to Apostasy

	Religiosity	Apostasy
Radicalism	.27	.25
Intellectualism	.16	.18
Maladjustment	.19	.18
Parental relations	.11	.12
Religiosity		.51

The first four germs show roughly the same degree of relationship to religiosity, the presumed intervening variable, as they do to apostasy, and by far the strongest association is that between religiosity and apostasy (.51). These correlations are roughly of the same order as the picture presented by the percentage tables.

Table 9.2 shows the path diagram linking the various germs to apostasy through religiosity. The diagram is set up on the assumption that the primary role of radicalism, intellectualism, maladjustment, and poor parental relations is to undermine religiosity, which in turn produces apostasy. This is somewhat of an oversimplification for, as we saw in Chapter 5, the absence of religiosity led to apostasy primarily when the other germs were present. The critical point about the coefficients presented in Table 9.2 is that they show the net effect of each variable on religiosity and on apostasy when the others are held constant.

Table 9.2: Path Analysis Linking Germs to Religiosity and Apostasy

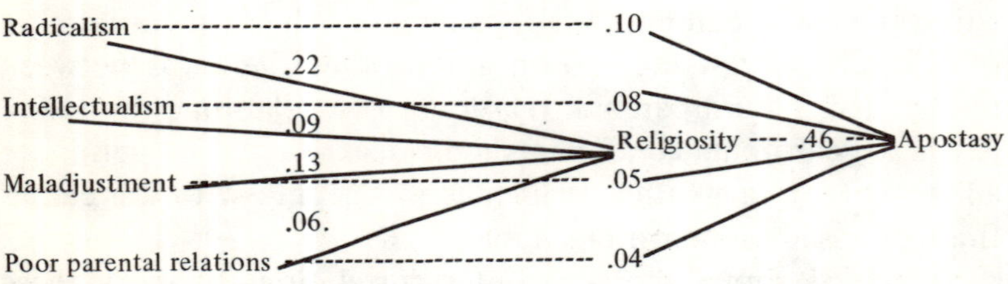

According to these coefficients, radicalism and maladjustment do more to undermine religiosity than intellectualism and poor parental relations. Of all the germs, "quality of parental relations" has the smallest net impact on both religiosity and apostasy. All the germs are more strongly related to religiosity than to apostasy when religiosity is taken into account, in keeping with the assumption that religiosity operates primarily as an intervening variable in the process leading to apostasy. But these results show that even when religiosity is held constant, the germs continue to show some relationship to apostasy, the coefficients ranging from a high of .10 for radicalism to a low of .04 for poor parental relations. Although small, these coefficients verify what we learned from the tabular analysis, namely that when religiosity is held constant, particularly among the nonreligious, the presence or absence of a germ is a significant factor in whether apostasy results. The path analysis thus tends to confirm the tabular analysis presented in the preceding chapters. Only religiosity is an overwhelming determinant of apostasy, but the other germs have their impact, first in undermining religiosity and then in generating apostasy in the absence of religiosity.

Similarities and Differences Among the Major Religions

A striking finding of the study was that whatever determined apostasy in one religion had the same effect in the other religions. Thus, the flow chart presented applies to Jews, Protestants, and Catholics. Nevertheless, there were significant differences among the three religions. The data showed that the religious identities of Protestants and Catholics rested much more on religious belief than did the identity of Jews. Jews had no difficulty identifying themselves as Jews even though they were not religious, indicating that Jewish identity rested heavily on the second pillar of identity, communality or ethnicity.

One major difference between the religions was that the Jews, much more than the Protestants and Catholics, had the "germs" of apostasy. Jews were much more likely than those raised in the other religions to have poor parental relations, to be committed to higher values, to have the symptoms of maladjustment, to be political radicals and, in particular, to be committed to intellectualism. Had the Protestants and Catholics possessed these germs to the same extent as the Jews, their apostasy rates would have soared far beyond that of the Jews. The relatively low Jewish rate of apostasy, in spite of their propensity for the germs of apostasy, is yet another indication of the importance of communality as a basis of Jewish identity. As expected, these germs did serve to lower Jewish religious commitment, but because of the dual basis for Jewish identity, most Jews retained their identity with the Jewish community in spite of their antireligious traits. At the other extreme, the

Protestants, adherents of the majority religion in America, were least likely to have the germs of apostasy and yet their apostasy rate was virtually the same as the Jewish rate in 1961. This can only indicate the weakness of the religious identity of Protestants. Were they to manifest the traits of apostasy to the same extent as the Jews, they would undoubtedly have a very high rate of apostasy.

The religions were found to differ in other respects. In Chapter 7 and again in Chapter 8, we examined data on the trends and stability of apostasy in the three religions. Both Protestants and Catholics showed an increase in apostasy over time. Between 1961 and 1964 and again between 1964 and 1968, the rate of apostasy increased in both the Protestant and Catholic groups. Moreover, once Protestants and Catholics opted for apostasy, they tended to stick to that position as relatively few Protestant and Catholic apostates returned to the fold in subsequent years. But the picture is quite different for the Jews. Unlike the Christians, the Jews did not show a trend toward apostasy over time. The rate of apostasy in 1961 among Jews was as high as it was three years later in 1964, and by 1968 the Jewish apostasy rate actually declined. Furthermore, the Jewish apostates demonstrated considerable instability. In subsequent years substantial numbers of them returned to the fold. In fact, so many Jewish apostates became identifiers at later points that they easily offset the new Jewish apostates, causing the overall Jewish apostasy rate to be quite stable. These sharp differences in both trends and stability of apostasy no doubt relate to the fundamental differences in the bases of Jewish identity compared with those of Protestants and Catholics.

Still another striking difference between the religions was the relatively low rate of apostasy among the Catholics in the 1961 study. The Catholic apostasy rate in 1961 was only half that of the Jews and the Protestants. In explaining this fact, we noted that a substantial number of Catholics received their education in Catholic colleges, and as the data revealed, hardly any Catholics attending Catholic colleges apostatized. But Catholics who attended secular schools, particularly the high-quality Ivy

League schools, did apostatize to the same degree as those in the other religions, if not more so. On the basis of the 1961 data we would have concluded that the Catholic community succeeded in holding its own by having developed parallel institutions that protected its children from the secularizing forces associated with higher education. But this solution to the continuity of the religious community was not without its dilemmas and perils. Basically, the quality of education offered at religiously controlled colleges, whether they be Protestant or Catholic, is substantially inferior to that offered by nonsectarian colleges and universities. Numerous studies of higher education have established this fact. For example, in the early fifties Lazarsfeld and Thielens surveyed college professors from over one hundred and fifty institutions and found that the denominational colleges were of substantially lower quality than the secular ones, and more recently the 1969 Carnegie study has come up with the same finding.[2]

This fact posed a serious dilemma for the minority religions of Catholicism and Judaism, the religions of America's ethnic communities, which in turn were the products of the massive waves of immigration. The requirements of upward mobility, the goal of the ethnics, more and more rested upon higher education and if the children of these ethnic groups were to achieve success, it became more and more imperative for them to receive a quality education. In short, the demands for continuity of the religious group came into conflict with the demands for upward mobility. The religiously controlled colleges found themselves at the heart of this dilemma. They either had to retain their religious purity and risk going out of business, or else they had to try to upgrade their quality by loosening the religiously doctrinaire controls over the institutions. In the sixties, a number of Catholic colleges, especially Notre Dame and Fordham, chose to become more secularized by allowing laymen on their boards of trustees and faculties, steps that these institutions felt were essential to upgrading their quality.[3]

With the data of the 1969 Carnegie study we now know how this fundamental dilemma has been resolved for the Catholics.

The pressures for upward mobility have apparently won out over the pressures for religious continuity. The number of Catholics seeking higher education has risen dramatically over the past decade or so, and the Catholic colleges have not expanded to absorb these aspirants, partly because the Catholic students have found secular institutions more attractive. As the Carnegie study demonstrated so clearly, over the eight-year period from 1961 to 1969, the Catholic apostasy rate caught up with those in the other religions. This process of catching up meant much more than matching the 1961 rates of the other religions, for as the comparative data show, apostasy increased dramatically in all three religions, a growth that, judging from the ACE data on incoming freshmen, is an inexorable process. In short, the 1969 apostasy rates for Jews, Protestants, and Catholics were substantially higher than in 1961, and by 1969 the forces making for apostasy were as effective among Catholics as among Protestants and Jews. The reason for the Catholics matching the apostasy of the Jews and Protestants is the breakdown of the Catholic college as the home of Catholic college students. Catholics now attend secular colleges in great numbers and are exposed to the same secularizing forces as are Jews and Protestants.

From the perspective of the religious communities in America, perhaps the most alarming data we have presented are the trends toward apostasy among entering college freshmen shown by the American Council on Education's annual surveys. Since these entering freshmen have not yet been exposed to the heady atmosphere of college, it is clear that the tendency toward apostasy has its roots in deeper sources within society than higher education. In short, the major religions would accomplish little if they banned their young from attending college, for although apostasy undoubtedly grows during the college years, as we tried to show in Chapter 6 and as the Carnegie data presented in Chapter 8 verified, it is also growing at a rather rampant rate among the young before they reach college. Were this trend to continue unchecked, it may well mean that in fifty years or so, America's religious communities as we know them today, will have disappeared.

What do the findings of this study have to say to the religious leaders concerned with the survival of their religious communities? Perhaps one basis for drawing inferences for action stems from the findings relating to the Jews. In spite of their propensity for the germs of apostasy, the overwhelming majority of Jews have little difficulty retaining their identity as Jews even though they are not religious. This is because Judaism represents a community, an ethnic tie, as well as a set of religious beliefs. Perhaps the Protestants and Catholics can strengthen their religions by building into them the components of communality, independent of religious doctrine. To some extent we are witnessing such a phenomenon today in Christianity with the spread of charismatic, pentacostalistic practices within the established churches. The charismatic movement is based not on new doctrine, but rather on new ways of expressing old faith, and the spirit of communality is very close to these new ways of religious expression. In fact, many adherents of the charismatic movement have come to experiment with communal living. The new religious revivals that have swept through the youth of America in the past several years, the "Jesus freaks," the followers of Maharaja Ji, the Children of God, and a host of other messianic cults, all have in common the emphasis on communality, including communal living.

How America's religious communities will evolve in the future remains to be seen. But in light of the strong trends toward apostasy, it would not be surprising if new forms of religious expression, embedded in a sense of community, did grow and flourish. The future may yet see the emergence of "secularized religions" that have their wellsprings in the psychic energy that is generated by communal life.

NOTES

1. Excluded from this analysis is "commitment to higher values," which previous findings showed is related to apostasy largely because of its heavy overlap with intellectualism.

2. See, Paul F. Lazarsfeld and Wagner Thielens, Jr., *The Academic Mind*, New York: Free Press, 1957.

3. Within the Jewish community, the one group that has rejected the goal of upward mobility in favor of religious purity and continuity of the religious community is the Chassidim. The Chassidim have actively discouraged their youth from attending secular colleges and they have sought to establish their own communities, separating themselves from those not of their faith. Needless to say, the great majority of Jews still stress upward mobility.

APPENDIX

THE CONVERTS

This report has been based entirely on two groups of students: those who were raised in one of the major religions and remained in that religion at the time of the survey and those who were raised in a major religion but had opted for no religion by the time of their graduation from college. Excluded were several groups of students, such as those raised in no religion or a minor religion and, most significantly, those who had converted to some other religion. Information on converts appeared only in Tables 1.2 and 8.10, where the proportion of converts as well as apostates in each religion was shown.

As the data of Table 1.2 showed, conversion is a rare phenomenon in American society. Among college seniors in the class of 1961, only 3 percent of those raised in one of the three major religions had converted (2 percent of those raised as Jews, 4 percent of the Protestants, and 3 percent of the Catholics).

One might expect that most conversions take place in adult life, after graduation from college, especially when one decides to marry out of his faith. But by 1964, the proportion of converts in the sample rose only to 5 percent (2 percent of the Jews, 6 percent of the Protestants, and 4 percent of the Catholics). This suggests that even when most of the graduates are married (as they were three years after graduation), conversion is still relatively rare.

The purpose of this appendix is to examine the determinants of conversion. This will be done from two perspectives. First, we shall compare the identifiers and apostates with the converts with regard to the apostasy germs in order to learn whether converts more closely resemble identifiers or apostates. Second, we shall present data on the role of intermarriage in the conversion process.

The Apostasy Traits and Conversion

Conversion of those raised in a minority religion like Judaism and, to a lesser extent, Catholicism, has been treated in the literature as part of the process of assimilation. Presumably, the Jew who converts to another religion takes on the attributes associated with adherents of the majority religion, i.e., Protestantism. With the data on hand, we can test the validity of this view. Some might argue that apostasy, the giving up of one's religion of origin, is merely a way station toward conversion, i.e., today's apostates are tomorrow's converts. The merits of this line of reasoning can also be tested with the data on hand.

To simplify the analysis, we shall compare identifiers, apostates and converts in each religion with regard to the apostasy germs, that is, the category of the attribute found to be most associated with apostasy, i.e., higher values, maladjustment, radicalism, poor parental relations, intellectuality, and nonreligiosity. Table A-1 compares identifiers, apostates and converts in each religion with respect to three of these traits. Because we are dealing with the data from wave 1, which did not contain the items used to measure quality of parental relations, we shall use an item strongly related to quality of parental relations, whether the graduate considered parental advice important when making a career decision. As shown in Chapter 2, apostates were much less likely than identifiers to attribute importance to parental advice. In addition to this item, Table A-1 shows the percentage high on "higher values" and the percentage of maladjusted among the identifiers, converts, and apostates in each religion.

Table A-1: A Comparison of Identifiers, Converts, and Apostates in Each Religion of Origin on Selected Traits Associated with Apostasy. (in percentages)

Current Status	Parental Advice Unimportant	High on "Higher Values"	Maladjusted
Jews			
Identifiers	32 (3,011)	25 (3,083)	17 (3,083)
Converts	52 (79)	41 (84)	21 (84)
Apostates	67 (460)	42 (465)	38 (465)
Protestants			
Identifiers	37 (1,545)	15 (15,958)	10 (15,958)
Converts	50 (730)	27 (761)	15 (761)
Apostates	59 (2,153)	28 (2,218)	25 (2,218)
Catholics			
Identifiers	36 (7,182)	18 (7,387)	12 (7,387)
Converts	49 (220)	22 (222)	18 (222)
Apostates	69 (551)	29 (566)	28 (566)

For all three of the apostasy traits shown in Table A-1, the converts in each religion fall in between the identifiers and the apostates, that is, they are more likely to possess the trait that undermines identification with the religious group of origin than the identifiers, but less so than the apostates. Significantly, the identifiers in each religion tend to be rather similar whatever the trait. The assimilationist theory of Jewish conversion is totally refuted by the fact that the Jewish converts are further removed from the Protestant identifiers than the Jewish identifiers. And rather than apostasy being a way station to conversion, these data suggest that the opposite may be more correct, that conversion is a step toward apostasy. Alienated from his religion of origin, the graduate may experiment with another religion before rejecting religion altogether. Converts clearly do not manifest the syndrome of religious identification to the same degree as those who retained their original identification.

These same patterns emerge when the other three apostasy traits dealt with earlier are considered, radicalism, commitment to an intellectual career and nonreligiosity. These findings appear in Table A-2.

Table A-2: A Comparison of Identifiers, Converts, and Apostates in Each Religion of Origin on Additional Traits Associated with Apostasy (in percentages)

Current Status	High on Radicalism	High on Intellectualism	Nonreligious
Jews			
Identifiers	11 (3,000)	6 (2,933)	33 (3,042)
Converts	25 (80)	14 (81)	31 (80)
Apostates	32 (458)	19 (454)	85 (458)
Protestants			
Identifiers	2 (15,502)	3 (15,170)	10 (15,797)
Converts	10 (737)	10 (720)	22 (750)
Apostates	13 (2,176)	13 (2,141)	67 (2,185)
Catholics			
Identifiers	4 (7,165)	3 (7,058)	4 (7,310)
Converts	10 (217)	7 (216)	21 (222)
Apostates	17 (550)	11 (544)	63 (550)

As in Table A-1, the identifiers are least likely to have the apostasy-provoking trait and the apostates are most likely to have it, with the converts in between. The patterns for radicalism and intellectuality are much like those for parental relations, higher values, and maladjustment in that the converts tend to be more similar to the apostates than the identifiers. But on the matter of religiosity, the converts, not surprisingly, since they identify with a religion, are much closer to the identifiers than to the apostates. Among Jews, converts are slightly *less* likely to be nonreligious than the identifiers; among Protestants and Catholics they are more likely than identifiers to be nonreligious but not nearly to the same extent as the apostates.

Intermarriage and Conversion

We are accustomed to viewing conversion as being generated in large part by intermarriage. Although intermarriage, as we shall see, is a factor in conversion, it is clearly not the decisive factor, for most of the converts in 1961 were neither married nor engaged. At the same time, the converts were more likely than the nonconverts to be married at that early date. By 1964, the role of intermarriage in the conversion process was more evident, as can be seen from Table A-3. In this table, identifiers, converts, and apostates in each religion are characterized by the type of marriage they have based on religion of origin and current religion. On the basis of religion of origin, they could have married endogamously or exogamously, i.e., a person raised in the same religion or a different religion. On the basis of current religion, their spouse could either adhere to their current position (including apostasy) which would represent endogamy, or their spouse could have a different religious status (exogamy). These combinations result in four types of marriage based on whether the marriage is exogamous or endogamous in terms of religion of origin or current religion. As Table A-3 shows, the great majority of converts in each religion, in contrast with identifiers and apostates, are involved in marriages that started out as exogamous on the basis of religion of origin, but are now endogamous because of the conversion of one spouse to the religion of another.

Table A-3: Original Marital Status By Current Marital Status Presented for Identifiers, Converts and Apostates in Each Religion (as of 1964, in percentages)

Marital Status Based on Religion of Origin	Endogamous	Endogamous	Exogamous	Exogamous	
Current Religion	Endogamous	Exogamous	Endogamous	Exogamous	
Religious Status, 1964					
Jews					
Identifiers	93	1	1	5	100 (1,245)
Converts	17	10	67	6	100 (30)
Apostates	26	24	35	15	100 (113)
Protestants					
Identifiers	88	1	4	7	100 (7,513)
Converts	17	14	63	6	100 (569)
Apostates	27	37	23	14	101 (862)
Catholics					
Identifiers	75	0	10	15	100 (2,453)
Converts	4	6	80	10	100 (161)
Apostates	9	14	46	31	100 (245)

In each religion, the great majority of the married identifiers have been consistently involved in endogamous marriages. The apostates, in contrast, tend to be spread out among the various types of marriages. It will be noted that in each religion a minority of apostates are characterized by consistently endogamous marriages. For apostates, this means that they married a person raised in their own original religion and that both partners currently have no religious identification. The key finding in the table is the fact that among the converts only, the great majority in each religion have shifted from exogamy to endogamy (column three). This clearly points to the role of conversion as a device for resolving intermarriages based on religion of origin.

This appendix has shown that the converts are not "holier than thou." Instead of resembling the adherents to the major religions, they are closer to the apostates. In fact, the identifiers in the three major religions are more similar to each other than they are to the converts to their religion. We have seen that intermarriage is a major force in the conversion process. Those who intermarry tend to reduce possible tensions by converting to the religion of their spouse. It is also possible that after converting, people tend to seek a marital partner from their new religion. Undoubtedly, both processes are at work. In either event, conversion and intermarriage are intimately entwined.

INDEX

ABOUT THE AUTHORS

DAVID CAPLOVITZ is Professor of Sociology at the Graduate Center of the City University of New York and prior to this he was affiliated with Columbia University. He is the author of *The Poor Pay More* (1963), *The Merchants of Harlem* (1973), and *Consumers in Trouble* (1974). Dr. Caplovitz is currently the recipient of a Guggenheim Award and is preparing a book on the impact of inflation on American families.

FRED SHERROW received his Ph.D. at Columbia University in 1971. His dissertation dealt with religious intermarriage. Dr. Sherrow was very active in Jewish Affairs in New York. He died in 1971.

ABOUT THE ASSISTANTS

STANLEY RAFFEL became Ph.D. from Columbia in 1972 and is currently teaching sociology in Scotland. STEVEN COHEN got his Ph.D., also from Columbia, in 1974 and is currently teaching at Queens College, the City University of New York.

ENNIS AND NANCY HAM LIBRARY
ROCHESTER COLLEGE
800 WEST AVON ROAD
ROCHESTER HILLS, MI 48307